Emotional Intelligence

Your Guide to Improving Social Skills, Building Happier Relationships, and Connecting Effortlessly

By: Dana Williams

Table of Contents

Introduction

Welcome to *Emotional Intelligence: Your Guide to Improving Social Skills, Building Happier Relationships, and Connecting Effortlessly.* The purpose of this book is to do exactly what the title states, and give you the necessary tools to:

- Improve Social Skills
- Build Happier Relationships
- Connect Effortlessly

You will also learn more about the idea of emotional intelligence and why it plays such a vital role in your life.

Chapter Layout

Each chapter in this book is divided into three sections:

- Learn
- Review
- Do

Learn

In this section you will learn the information about each chapter's topic. This is where you will find an in-depth discussion on the subject, and where all of the concepts will be introduced.

Review

In this section you will find a list of the top ten ideas to remember about what you just learned.

Do

In this section you will find specific activities and exercises to reinforce the topic and help you put what you learned into action.

Now that you know the layout, let's get started! In the first chapter, you will learn all about emotional intelligence. You will see examples of what it looks like and how emotional intelligence is different than other forms of intelligence. You will also get a brief explanation of the history of the field and the four main areas in which emotional intelligence is measured.

Chapter 1: What Is Emotional Intelligence?

"I don't want to be at the mercy of my emotions. I want to use them, to enjoy them, and to dominate them." — *Oscar Wilde*

Learn

As you navigate through life, you will learn and develop in many areas. You will develop several different types of intelligence, and strengthening your emotional intelligence is one of the most important things you can do.

Before diving into emotional intelligence, let's take a quick look at the different types of basic intelligence.

Types of Intelligence

In 1983, Harvard Psychologist Howard Gardner developed the theory of multiple intelligences. He realized that people do not exhibit just one form of intelligence, and that if a person is lower than average in one ability, it does not necessarily mean they lack intelligence; it could just mean their intelligence lies in a different area.

Gardner determined there were eight different types of intelligence:

- Logical-mathematical
- Linguistic

- Spatial
- Musical
- Bodily-kinesthetic
- Intrapersonal
- Interpersonal
- Naturalistic

Take a moment to familiarize yourself with each intelligence.

Logical-Mathematical
People with a high level of logical-mathematical intelligence tend to be skilled at solving problems, analyzing situations, and manipulating numbers. This intelligence not only correlates to a higher-than-average mathematical ability, but it also signifies a person's ability to use logic and reason. Those who exhibit logical-mathematical intelligence tend to choose careers in science, mathematics, engineering, computer programming, or accounting.

Linguistic
Linguistic intelligence refers to someone's ability to use words. Whether speaking or writing, a person with higher-than-average linguistic intelligence will be able to manipulate words for maximum effect. High linguistic intelligence typically indicates a strong memory, a broad sense of humor, and the ability to persuade or debate. Education, law, and journalism are very common career choices for those with linguistic intelligence.

Spatial

Spatial intelligence is also referred to as visual-spatial intelligence. This intelligence indicates the ability to visualize things, and typically indicates the ability to read maps, charts, and pictures. Those who have high levels of spatial intelligence often choose a career as an artist, architect, or engineer.

Musical

Musical intelligence involves the ability to think in sounds and rhythm. Someone with strong musical intelligence will often be able to compose and perform music and will have a deep appreciation for music. Career choices for someone strong in musical intelligence include singing, conducting, teaching music, or composing.

Bodily-Kinesthetic

Someone high in bodily-kinesthetic intelligence will generally have acute body awareness and will be able to move in ways that others cannot, such as when dancing or participating in sports. Bodily-kinesthetic intelligence usually indicates hand-eye coordination, physical strength, and a desire to be on the move in one way or another. Actors, body builders, and dancers are generally higher than average in bodily-kinesthetic intelligence.

Intrapersonal

Intrapersonal intelligence refers to an individual's ability to be aware of and understand his or her own emotions. A person with an abundance of intrapersonal intelligence will generally enjoy reflecting on their hopes and wishes, their strengths and weaknesses, and their relationships. Careers for those with intrapersonal intelligence include working as a scientist, a writer, or a philosopher.

Interpersonal

Someone with high interpersonal intelligence is typically skilled at interacting with other people and building and maintaining relationships. He or she will be able to read and understand the feelings and emotions of those with whom they interact. High interpersonal intelligence usually correlates to a better that average ability to communicate and resolve conflicts. Those who are strong in interpersonal intelligence may choose a career as a counselor, psychologist, or in sales.

Naturalistic

A person who feels connected with nature and is very aware of their surroundings is most likely high in naturalistic intelligence. Individuals with naturalistic intelligence may enjoy studying zoology or biology, and they will very likely enjoy being outdoors as often as possible. Gardeners, farmers, and conservationists are usually all very high in naturalistic intelligence.

Where does Emotional Intelligence fit in?

As you have most likely noticed, emotional intelligence is not one of the eight intelligences identified by Howard Gardner. So where does it fit in?

Peter Salovey and John D. Mayer

In 1990, Peter Salovey and John D. Mayer, two psychologists, published an article entitled *Emotional Intelligence*. In it, they defined emotional intelligence as a person's ability to not only understand his or her own emotions and feelings, but also the feelings and emotions of others. It is a blending of Gardner's intrapersonal and interpersonal intelligences.

Salovey and Mayer developed a test to identify and measure emotional intelligence. The test, the Mayer-Salovey-Caruso Emotional Intelligence Test (MSCEIT) measures these four areas of emotional intelligence:

- Emotional Perception – This measures how well you can perceive the emotions that you are experiencing, as well as the emotions of those around you. This includes characters in books or movies, as well as messages conveyed in songs or artwork.
- Thought Facilitation – This measures how well you can determine which emotions are appropriate for certain situations, and how well you can get yourself into an emotional state of being.
- Emotional Understanding – This measures how well you can understand emotions, and how they work to impact relationships and day-to-day living.
- Emotional Management – This measures how well you can manage and control your emotions, and how you can help others regulate their emotions.

Although Salovey and Mayer's theory is not as well-known as Gardner's, they made a profound impact in the study of emotional intelligence.

Daniel Goleman

In 1992, Daniel Goleman was researching emotional intelligence and found the article written by Salovey and Mayer. He asked them for permission to use the term, and in 1995 he published a book entitled *Emotional Intelligence*. His book became a best seller, and he appeared on television talk shows to promote his book.

Although there was some controversy over Goleman's book, with some experts saying that he made the subject too broad and took the focus off simply emotional intelligence, Goleman made a profound impact on the field. In 1998 he published another book, *Working with Emotional Intelligence,* and to this day there is much studied and written about emotional intelligence.

Now that you know the brief history of the field, let's take a look at the basic foundations of emotional intelligence.

Hallmarks of Emotional Intelligence

Salovey and Mayer determined that emotional intelligence can be broken down into four main areas: self-awareness, self-management, social awareness, and social skills.

Self-Awareness

Self-awareness is the ability to recognize the emotions you feel when you feel them. Self-awareness also allows you to manage your emotions. Developing this skill will help you know when you are walking into a situation that may be difficult for you and will help you be able to face and process disappointments.

Self-awareness also includes the concept of self-confidence and self-esteem. It involves knowing your worth and recognizing what you are capable of. It means getting to the point where you can accept and acknowledge your own thoughts and feelings, and you do not look to others for validation.

Self-Management

Self-management is the ability to gain control over your emotions. You do not know when your emotions are going to come up. There is a lot that happens in life that you cannot control. You are going to face distressing situations, and there are going to be times when you are sad and upset. Self-management is your ability to handle yourself during these times and not let your emotions control you.

Self-management also indicates your ability to hold yourself to a high standard and live a life of integrity. You make wise choices, are trustworthy, and strive to do your best and be your best in every situation. A byproduct of this skill is added confidence, as you know that you can handle yourself no matter what comes your way.

Social Awareness

Social awareness involves not only being aware of what is going on around you, but also having empathy for other people. You anticipate the needs of people and do what you can to try to meet those needs. You know if someone needs to talk, and you know how to truly listen when they do speak. You also know if someone would rather sit and be quiet, and you are comfortable with silence.

Social awareness also means you can read the interactions between people and pick up on group dynamics. You can figure out the balance of power in a relationship or group setting and learn how to function according to the unwritten rules that may be in play.

Social Skills

To put it simply, social skills are your ability to interact with others. It means being able to talk with people, break the ice, and handle confrontation. As you develop stronger social skills, you will become more assertive, more influential, and will most likely find yourself taking on leadership roles in a wide variety of situations, both intentionally and unintentionally.

Review

Here are the top ten things to remember about emotional intelligence:

1. In 1983, Howard Gardner developed the Theory of Multiple Intelligences.
2. Gardner identified eight different intelligences. These intelligences include: Logical-mathematical, Linguistic, Spatial, Musical, Bodily-kinesthetic, Intrapersonal, Interpersonal, and Naturalistic.
3. In 1990, Peter Salovey and John D. Mayer introduced the concept of emotional intelligence, which is a combination of Gardner's idea of Interpersonal and Intrapersonal intelligences.
4. Salovey and Mayer created a test to assess an individual's emotional intelligence. The test measures emotional perception, thought facilitation, emotional understanding, and emotional management.

5. In 1992, Daniel Goleman wrote a book on emotional intelligence and brought the topic into popular discussion.
6. There are four main hallmarks of emotional intelligence: self-awareness, self-management, social awareness, and social skills.
7. Self-awareness involves recognizing your own emotions. It also involves having self-esteem, self-confidence, and self-worth.
8. Self-management involves learning to manage your emotions and not letting them control you. It also involves holding yourself to a high standard and aiming to be trustworthy.
9. Social awareness involves knowing what people around you may be experiencing and having empathy for them. It also involves being aware of the interactions between people and understanding and reading group dynamics.
10. Social skills refer to your ability to interact with people and how you handle yourself in a wide range of situations.

Do

Before you move on to the next chapter, take some time to reflect on what you have learned and consider the following questions.

1. As you think about Howard Gardner's multiple intelligences, which one do you feel is your strongest?
2. As you think about Gardner's theory, which intelligence is your weakest?

3. Are you currently in a career, or are you pursuing a career, which utilizes your strengths? If yes, was this intentional? If no, why not?
4. As you consider the Mayer-Salovey-Caruso Emotional Intelligence Test (MSCEIT), which of the four components do you feel is your strongest?
5. Which component of the MSCEIT do you feel you need to work on the most?
6. When you read about the four hallmarks of emotional intelligence, which do you feel is your greatest strength?
7. Which hallmark of emotional intelligence is your weakness?
8. Why are you reading this book?
9. What changes would you like to see in your life after reading this book?
10. Name one person you can share your journey with. Consider telling them about the book, what you would like to see happen from reading the book, and what areas you are going to focus on.

As we shift our focus solely to emotional intelligence, we will begin by looking at your brain and what is going on inside your head. In the next chapter you will learn how your brain works. You will discover which parts of your brain are responsible for different components of your thought process, language development and production, and even vision.

Chapter 2: How Does It Work?

"The human brain has 100 billion neurons, each neuron connected to 10,000 other neurons. Sitting on your shoulders is the most complicated object in the known universe." — *Michio Kaku*

Have you ever stopped to consider all that your brain does? It is such a small organ, yet it is what keeps you functioning day in and day out. Your brain controls everything. It controls what you think and feel, how you hear or see things, what you remember, and even how you sit.

When it comes to developing emotional intelligence, it is important to start by understanding what happens in your brain, because that is where it all takes place. Once you learn the physiology behind what is happening, it will very likely be easier to know how to make changes and adjustments.

Learn

You know that your brain sits inside your head, but let's take a closer look at the makeup of your brain.

Anatomy of the Brain

Your brain is comprised of three main sections: cerebrum, cerebellum, and brainstem. Each section is responsible for different functions.

- Cerebrum – The cerebrum is the largest part of your brain. This is the part of your brain that controls things such as speech, learning, emotions, and reasoning. It is where you process hearing, vision, and touch. Your cerebrum is divided into two parts, the right and left hemispheres. You may have heard these referred to as your right brain and left brain.

     In the past, scientists theorized that people tend to have one side of the cerebrum that is more developed than the other, but recent research has proved that both sides develop and function the same, and they work together. There is a network of fibers between the two sides of your cerebrum that move messages back and forth from one side to the other. An interesting fact about the hemispheres is that the right hemisphere controls the left side of your body, and the left hemisphere controls the right side of your body. Each hemisphere has its own functions:

     o Right Brain – Your right brain is often considered the creative part of your brain. It is not very organized, and it processes visual cues. This is the part of your brain responsible for daydreaming, imagination, art, and intuition.
     o Left Brain – Your left brain is the more organized and analytical part of your brain. It is often considered more logical and verbal, and it is believed to be the part of your brain

that processes the concepts of math, facts, logic, and words.

Differences in personality or interests, such as those who are drawn to art rather than mathematics, or music rather than writing, don't necessarily have a stronger or more developed right brain; they just have different preferences and personalities.

- Cerebellum – The cerebellum is nestled just underneath the cerebrum. It is the part of your brain that keeps you moving, standing, and balanced. It controls the movement of your muscles, your balance, and your posture.

- Brainstem – As the name suggests, your brainstem sits at the bottom of your brain. It connects the other two parts of the brain to the spinal cord. This is the part of your brain that is responsible for all of the functions you do automatically, without thinking. For example, digestion, breathing, and heart rate are all controlled by the brain stem.

Functions of the Brain

You have learned that your cerebrum is divided into two hemispheres. Each one of those hemispheres is then divided into four lobes. These are the frontal lobe, parietal lobe, occipital lobe, and temporal lobe. The lobes all control different processes, but they all work together and are connected.

- Frontal Lobe – Your frontal lobe controls a wide range of functions. It is responsible for your behavior, emotions, and personality. It is also where you work on problem solving, as well as making plans and judgments. In addition, your frontal lobe is the location of your self-awareness, concentration, and intelligence, and it is also where you will find the specific areas that control speech, writing, and movement.

- Parietal Lobe – The parietal lobe contains the area that moderates your temperature and controls your senses of pain and touch. It is also where you interpret language that you hear, and where you process words. Your parietal lobe is the processing and interpreting center for all of your senses and memory.
- Occipital Lobe – Your occipital lobe is all about vision. This is where you interpret different colors, as well as movement and light.
- Temporal Lobe – Although you hear and process language in different lobes, the temporal lobe is what contains the features necessary to understand language. It is also responsible for hearing, memory, and organizing.

When it comes to language, the vast majority of the work is done in the left hemisphere in two specific areas: Broca's Area and Wernicke's Area.

- Broca's Area – Broca's area is in your left frontal lobe. This is the part of the brain that allows you to actually form words. It controls the movement of your lips, tongue, and jaw. It also controls your breathing while you are speaking, allowing you to form different words.

18

- Wernicke's Area – Wernicke's area is in your left temporal lobe. This is the part of the brain that allows you to understand words and put them together to form coherent sentences.

In addition to the areas you have already learned about, there are three other structures that control very specific and necessary operations. These are the motor strip, the sensory strip, and the cortex.

- Motor Strip – The motor strip is in the back part of your frontal lobe and is responsible for movement. The motor strip in your left frontal lobe is responsible for the movement on the right side of your body, and the motor strip in your right frontal lobe is responsible for movement on the left side of your body.
- Sensory Strip – Your sensory strip is what takes care of sending all of the messages about senses and feelings from one part of the body to another. It is located in your parietal lobe.
- Cortex – Your cortex is the surface of your cerebrum. This is the part of your brain that looks like a series of bumps and folds. There are sixteen billion neurons on the cortex. The nerve cells are what give your brain the greyish color and why this part of your brain is called grey matter. Right underneath the cortex lie all of the fibers that connect all of the parts of the brain together, and this area is called white matter.

Finally, there are several other structures in the brain that help control every part of living. Three of these structures are your hypothalamus, your pituitary gland, and your thalamus.

- Hypothalamus – Your hypothalamus is in control of your autonomic system. This includes your basic bodily functions like sleep, thirst, hunger, and sexual response. This is where your blood pressure, temperature, hormones, and emotions are regulated.

- Pituitary Gland – Your pituitary gland is located at the base of your skull. It is connected to your hypothalamus, and it controls all of the endocrine glands in your body. It releases hormones that help you respond to stress, encourage muscle and bone development, and regulate sexual development.

- Thalamus – Your thalamus is responsible for relaying information. It takes all of the information that comes in and out of your cortex and sends the information where it needs to go.

Memory

Several parts of your brain are involved when it comes to memory. There are three distinct processes you go through related to memory: encoding, storing, and recalling. In the encoding stage, your brain processes all of the information and decides what is important and needs to be retained. Then it stores the memory, either in long-term or short-term memory. Recalling is what occurs when you access these memories and bring them back into the focus of your attention.

You have three different types of memory, and all three are processed in different areas of your brain. The three types of memory are short-term memory, long-term memory, and skill memory.

- Short-Term Memory – Your short-term memory is processed in your prefrontal cortex. This is also called your working memory, and it only stores information for one minute. It is limited to just about seven items. This is what helps you remember a phone number you just heard. It is also used when you are reading, to help you remember what is happening from sentence to sentence.

- Long-Term Memory – Your long-term memory is processed in your temporal lobe, in an area called the hippocampus. This is the area that you use when you want to remember something for longer than a minute. There is no limit to its capacity, and this is where you store such things as facts, number calculations, and all of your personal recollections and memories.

- Skill Memory – Your skill memory is processed in your cerebellum. This is where you store the information that you need to perform basic skills, such as playing the piano, tying your shoe, or riding a bike.

Review

Here are the top ten things to remember about how your brain works.

1. Your brain is divided into three main areas: the cerebellum, cerebrum, and brainstem.
2. Your cerebrum is divided into left and right hemispheres. The left hemisphere controls the right side of your body, and the right hemisphere controls the left side of your body.
3. Each hemisphere is divided into four lobes: the frontal lobe, parietal lobe, occipital lobe, and temporal lobe.
4. Your frontal lobe is responsible for behavior, emotions, and personality.
5. Your parietal lobe is the processing center for all of your senses and memory.
6. Your occipital lobe is responsible for vision.
7. Your temporal lobe is responsible for hearing, memory, and learning.
8. Broca's area and Wernicke's area are responsible for everything that has to do with speech. Broca's area controls the physical behaviors you need to speak, and Wernicke's area is where you comprehend words and form them into sentences.
9. The cortex is the surface of your brain. It contains sixteen billion neurons and is referred to as grey matter.
10. You have three different types of memory: short-term memory, long-term memory, and skill memory. Your short-term memory stores information for about a minute and can hold around seven items at a time. Your long-term memory has no maximum capacity. Your skill memory is where you retain all of the information necessary to perform different tasks.

Do

Try these activities to reinforce what you have just learned about your brain.

Picture It

Print out or draw a diagram of your brain. Label each section, and list one or two things that each section is responsible for. Put the picture somewhere that it can be easily accessed and commit to spending five to ten minutes every day studying it. Every day, cover up one or two of the labels, and eventually you will have learned where everything is.

Notice It

As you go throughout your day, take note of the different activities that you are doing and acknowledge which part of your brain is responsible for what is happening. For example, as you read, think about the fact that it is your short-term memory helping you remember the previous sentence. As you tie your shoes, consider the fact it is your skill memory that holds the information to help you tie your shoes. As you speak, acknowledge that Wernicke's area is helping you form the sentences, while Broca's area is helping you form the words. By paying attention to this, you will not only learn and have a greater appreciation for your brain, but you will also begin to practice mindfulness, which plays a very large part in Emotional Intelligence. You will learn more about mindfulness in a later chapter.

Now that you have a better understanding of your brain in general, it is time to get down to specifically focusing on emotions and emotional intelligence. In the next chapter we will discuss what happens, both physically and emotionally, when you get upset or triggered. You will see that although there are some reactions you can control, there are others that happen automatically. You will also learn very specific exercises you can do to help keep your emotions under control when you are in crisis.

Chapter 3: What Happens When You Get Triggered?

"The amygdala in the emotional center sees and hears everything that occurs to us instantaneously and is the trigger point for the fight or flight response." — Daniel Goleman

Learn

Getting triggered: We have all been there. Something happens or someone says something and, for a lack of a better term, we lose it. We get upset, maybe we yell or scream, or we say things without even thinking. On the other hand, sometimes we just want to get away. We want to run from the situation, or perhaps we want to even run away from everyone. There may be other situations where we just freeze. We completely shut down, and we don't know what to do next.

Why does this happen? What can we do about it?

Fight or Flight

When you encounter something that frightens you, your body automatically goes into what is called the acute stress response. This is also called the fight or flight response. In this situation, your body prepares for you to do one of two things: You will either fight whatever is frightening you, or you will run away from the situation.

When you think about prehistoric life, people frequently faced life-threatening dangers. If they encountered a wild animal, they immediately had to fight the animal or run away from it. This is where the fight or flight response helped them survive. Their bodies were prepared to help them, no matter what choice they made. They were ready for the challenge, both physically and mentally.

Although getting chased by a wild animal is no longer a common threat for the majority of us, we still have the fight or flight response. Studies have shown that this response is activated not only in the presence of physical danger, but also in the presence of psychological danger. When you face a sudden and extreme stressor, your body goes through specific changes to help you prepare to act.

- Hormones – The first thing that happens when you face severe stress is that your body releases hormones called adrenaline and noradrenaline. This causes your blood pressure, heart rate, and rate of breathing to increase.
- Pupils Dilate – When you are in this response, your pupils dilate. This lets more light into your eyes and helps you have a better look at everything around you.
- Skin Changes Color – Sometimes you will get very pale during the fight-or-flight response, and sometimes you will get flushed. This happens because when your body thinks you are in danger, it will send more of your blood to your muscles and send less blood to the

surface of your skin. The blood will also rush to your brain to help you make decisions faster.

- Heart and Breathing Rates Increase – This allows your body to take in more oxygen to get more energy. Your body is preparing to take action, and it is doing what it needs to do to make sure you can survive whatever happens.
- Body Trembling – When your muscles are tensed up and ready to act, they can start to shake. The trembling is not a psychological or intentional reaction to fear. It is a sign that your muscles are ready to work.

As you can see, when you are truly in danger, the fight or flight response is exactly what you need. However, there are times when the response kicks in simply because you *think* there is danger, even though none exists. You may also be enduring a chronically stressful situation, so your fight or flight response is almost always activated. Remember, this is supposed to help for a short time, until you are safe. Your body is not designed to live in a constant state of being ready to fight or flee at any time.

Amygdala Hijack

Amygdala hijack is a term that is used to describe what happens when stress causes your amygdala to take over and "hijack" your emotional responses. As you learned in the previous chapter, your frontal lobes are where your emotions are processed, where you think reasonably and logically, and where you are able to make plans. You control all of the actions that happen in your frontal lobe, and you are completely aware of what is happening.

When you believe there is danger nearby, whether physical or psychological danger, your amygdala wants to take over. It wants to launch the fight or flight response and handle the problem immediately. While this is happening, your frontal lobes are assessing the information to see if there really is danger, and what would be the best and most logical way to go about dealing with the issue at hand.

If your frontal lobes rationalize the danger is not severe, they overpower what the amygdala is trying to do. You are able to respond calmly, and your actions are rational and reasonable. However, if the danger is severe, your amygdala completely takes over, and it actually overpowers the frontal lobes. Your fight-or-flight response is activated, and your reactions and actions are not coming from a place of logic or control. You are acting on instinct.

While amygdala hijack is helpful in a truly life-threatening situation, you can imagine how it can cause problems when it is activated by a psychological danger or severe stress. You will react to situations in an intense, immediate, and irrational manner. Your amygdala has hijacked your mind, and you are unable to respond logically.

Reversing the Response
When your fight-or-flight response is activated, it is an automatic response to fear. If you suddenly feel this

28

response happening, there is nothing you can do to convince your brain that the fear isn't real. You are not thinking rationally, and if you try and reason with yourself, you will only make the situation worse.

The best thing to do is to reverse the response. As you intentionally calm down the physical response to danger, your body will sense that things are safer, and your brain will get the signal that it is time to relax.

There are a few different things you can do to reverse the response or interrupt the amygdala hijack. Read through the following exercises, and practice doing them now, when you are not in the middle of turmoil. The more you practice these when you are not overly stressed, the easier it will be to use them when you are overly stressed.

ABC

For this exercise you will take three very specific and deliberate actions to help you get back in control of the situations.

A – Acknowledge - Acknowledge what is happening. Admit that you feel angry, stressed, or threatened, and that your amygdala is trying to make you fight or flee. Remember that what is happening to you now, whether it is your heart pounding or your body trembling, is an automatic response. It does not mean you are truly in danger; it simply means your body is doing its job.

B – Breathe - Your breathing rate speeds up during the fight-or-flight response. By intentionally slowing your breathing, your body will sense that things are calm. Although you most likely have heard the advice to take a deep breath when you are upset, it would be more accurate to say take an intentional breath. This means thinking about every part of the breath. As you breathe in, imagine the air filling your lungs. Hold it for a few seconds, and imagine your body getting to work on taking in the oxygen. Then slowly let your breath out, feeling your shoulders relax as you do so. Take five intentional breaths, and then re-assess to see where you are. If you are able to start making rational thoughts, move on to the last step of this exercise. If you are still on high alert, take five more intentional breaths, and then re-assess.

C – Counter - Now that you are thinking calmly and rationally, it is time to address the perceived danger. The quickest way to do this is to find a counterexample to whatever it is that you fear. If you can find one counterexample, you will realize that the threat is not real, and you can move forward. Here are some examples:

> Fear: *Everyone hates me, and I am going to spend the rest of my life alone.*
> Counter: My friend Charles enjoys spending time with me, and there are others as well.
>
> Fear: *This person is going to yell at me.*
> Counter: Even if this person yells at me, I know who I am and I will be able to handle myself in an appropriate manner.

Fear: *I won't be able to get all of my work done.*
Counter: I had a huge project last week and I got that finished. I can ask for help if I need to.

Fear: *Nothing good will ever happen to me.*
Counter: I had a wonderful cup of coffee this morning. It was a small thing, but it was good, and more good things will happen to me.

Fear: *I can't do anything right.*
Counter: I intentionally made the choice to stop the amygdala hijack, and that is a good decision.

Fear: *My spouse is going to leave me, and I won't ever be loved again.*
Counter: I am a loveable person. Even if my spouse leaves me, I am strong and I will be able to endure it.

Fear: *I will lose my job and become destitute.*
Counter: Just last week my boss complimented my work. Additionally, even if I do lose my job, I will look for another one. If things get really bad, I can find a roommate, ask someone for a loan, or seek out ways to get financial assistance.

Countering the negative thoughts will help you give a more rational view of what is happening. You can then begin formulating a plan to improve your situation.

5-4-3

In this exercise, you will activate your different senses to help you focus on the present. You will pay attention to what is happening this very moment, and you will start to relax as you realize that you are not in immediate danger.

5 – Look around and name five things that you see. Label each one individually. For example, "I see a book. I see a pen. I see a picture. I see a mug. I see a table."
4 – Close your eyes and name four things you feel. For example, "I feel my watch on my wrist. I feel the wind in my face. I feel the softness of my shirt. I feel my shoes on my feet."
3 – With your eyes still closed, name three things you hear. For example, "I hear a clock ticking. I hear a car driving by. I hear myself breathing."

Once you have gone through all of these, take three intentional breaths. By this time, you should be more focused on what is real and in front of you. This will allow you to logically address your concerns.

Head to Toe

When your fight-or-flight response is activated, blood flows to your muscles and your body is prepared to act. By intentionally working and then relaxing each of your muscles, your brain will receive the signal that it is okay to be still.

Begin at the top of your head and work your way down your body all the way to your toes. The goal is to contract each of your major muscle groups, and then relax them. Take a deep breath in each time you contract your muscles, and slowly exhale as you relax.

- Eyes – Squeeze your eyes shut as tightly as you can, then open them.
- Mouth – Open your mouth as wide as you can, then slowly close your mouth.
- Shoulders – Pull your shoulders up toward your ears, and then lower them.
- Arms – Tighten your biceps as you curl your arms up toward you, and then slowly lower them.
- Hands – Make a fist with each hand and squeeze as tightly as you can, then slowly open your hand.
- Legs – Stand on your tiptoes to tighten your calf muscles, and then slowly lower back down.
- Toes – Curl your toes under, and then release them.

Once you have worked all of these muscle groups, take another deep, intentional breath. You should notice that you feel more relaxed and better able to tackle whatever you have to face.

Slow It Down

When your amygdala takes over, one of the best things that you can do is slow down. Your body is preparing to fight or flee, and by slowing down you can override the instinct and convince your amygdala that there is nothing to panic over, and it is okay to stand down. Try several of the different options to deliberately slow down:

33

- Take a slow, deep breath and slowly close your eyes. Count to five, and then slowly open your eyes again.
- Slowly change positions. If you are standing, slowly lower yourself into a sitting position. Do not flop down in a chair, but instead lower yourself as slowly as you can into the sitting position. If you are sitting, slowly stand to your feet.
- Take a slow, deliberate walk around the room. Take one step forward, breathe, and then take another step forward.
- Slowly extend your arms in front of you, and then bring them back toward you. Count to ten as you push your arms away, and then count to ten again as you bring them back in.
- If you are taking a drink of water, spend as much time as you can getting the cup to your lips. Then take a long, slow sip, and slowly lower the cup again.
- Slowly speak out loud. Repeat the words, "I am safe. There is no reason to panic." Draw the words out for as long as you can, focusing on each word as you say it.

Review

Here are the top ten things to remember about what happens when you get triggered.

1. The fight-or-flight response is also known as the acute stress response.
2. During times of severe stress, your body is flooded with hormones such as adrenaline and noradrenaline.

3. When you perceive extreme danger, the fight-or-flight response takes over and prepares your body to either fight whatever means to harm you or flee from whatever means to harm you.
4. The fight-or-flight response is automatic, and it is not something you can control.
5. Your emotions and thoughts are controlled and regulated in the frontal lobes. When you are experiencing the acute stress response, your amygdala takes over and momentarily overrides the functioning of your frontal lobes, making rational and logical thought unavailable. This situation is known as amygdala hijack.
6. Although there is no way to control the fight-or-flight response or amygdala hijack, there are ways to reverse the response and help your brain understand that you are not in true danger.
7. Taking intentional breaths can help calm an amygdala hijack. As your breathing slows, your mind will relax a bit. Your frontal lobes can then take charge again, and you can react rationally and appropriately to different situations.
8. Providing one counterexample to a frightening thought can help you gain a new perspective on the situation.
9. Intentionally activating your senses to pay attention to the present will help calm the fight-or-flight response. It will help focus on the present and will help you understand what is real versus the danger you imagine.
10. Although the fight-or-flight response and amygdala hijack are helpful in true life-or-death situations, they

can cause problems when they are activated due to psychological or emotional stress. Learning ways to manage these responses is essential for having high emotional intelligence.

Do

It is essential that you practice the different techniques for reversing an amygdala hijack. If you wait until you are in the middle of response to try these out, you will not be successful. Set aside time every day to practice all three of the exercises.

For the ABC exercise, start making a list of the different fears you know are a struggle for you, and find the counterexample for the fears. Again, do not do this only when you are upset. Find a time when you are relaxed and start writing them down. Keep the list handy, and when you are struggling, look at the list to remind you of the counterexamples to your fears.

Now that you understand what happens when you get upset and have learned some techniques for stopping amygdala hijack and the fight-or-flight response, it is time to discuss the benefits of strengthening your emotional intelligence. In the next chapter you will learn what you have to gain from putting in all of the hard work to learn and grow. You will see the benefits to you personally, as well as the benefits in the workplace and in an educational environment.

Chapter 4: Is It Worth It?

"In the last decade or so, science has discovered a tremendous amount about the role emotions play in our lives. Researchers have found that even more than IQ, your emotional awareness and abilities to handle feelings will determine our success and happiness in all walks of life, including family relationships." — John Gottman

Learn

Developing a strong emotional intelligence is not easy. It will take time and dedication, and it requires you to take an honest assessment of yourself. You may find that you discover things you don't like, and you will most likely feel uncomfortable at times throughout the process.

But is it worth it? Is it worth spending all of the time and effort this will require? The simple answer is yes, it is worth it. But that will not be enough to push you through when it gets really difficult.

Let's take a closer look at the issue so you can see just how much you will benefit from improving your emotional intelligence.

Risks of Neglecting Emotional Intelligence

One of the best ways to determine if something is worth it or not is to ask yourself what happens if you don't do it. When it comes to emotional intelligence, you need to understand that there are definite risks to neglecting this part of your life. You will see negative effects in your personal relationships, in business settings, and in academic settings.

Personal Relationships

Neglecting your emotional intelligence can wreak havoc in your personal relationships. You will notice some, if not all, of the following issues.

- Difficulty understanding what your loved ones are feeling. In any relationship, it is important to be able to have at least some understanding of what the other person is feeling. Although you may not know exactly what they are going through, having emotional intelligence allows you to be able to connect with them more and know them better. Not having this ability will make you seem as if you don't care what they are going through, and it will leave your loved one feeling neglected and alone. You will find that you fight more often, and you will have a difficult time truly connecting.

- Difficulty expressing yourself. If you do not understand your own emotions, you will not be able to effectively communicate your thoughts and feelings with someone else. You may realize that you don't feel exactly right, but if you cannot identify your emotions, you cannot help the other person understand what you are going through or how they can best help or support you. You will most likely both feel frustrated and will also very likely have more arguments and disagreements than you would if you could simply tell the other person how you are feeling. Additionally, if you do not understand what you are feeling, you will struggle to ask for what you need and get the help you need. Rather than moving forward and growing, you will constantly be trying to figure out what is going on inside your mind.

- Difficulty recognizing appropriate and inappropriate conversation topics. Not having a high level of emotional intelligence can cause you to offend those around you. If you are unaware that a particular topic is upsetting someone, you may forge ahead with a conversation that leaves the other person feeling uncomfortable or even hurt. You are not intentionally hurting them, but the pain is real. You may even begin to lose friends, as people may not feel comfortable around you.

- Difficultly reading body language. A lot can be discerned just by watching someone's body language. If they are folding their arms and pulling away from you, they are most likely uncomfortable and trying to physically separate themselves from the conversation. If you are not aware of this, and are unable to correctly read their cues, you will likely forge ahead in the conversation, making them feel even more uncomfortable. This person will most likely try to avoid you in the future.

In order to have positive and fulfilling relationships, both people in the relationship need to be able to recognize, validate, and accept the emotions of the other person. They do not always need to agree on issues, but each person needs to have the freedom and safety to think and feel whatever they think and feel. Neglecting your emotional intelligence will not only hurt the people around you, but it will also hurt you and cause you to miss out on some important life experiences.

Business Settings

Emotional intelligence plays a vital role within business settings. Neglecting your emotional intelligence can cause adverse side effects in your workplace, and can hurt your career growth and your earning potential. It can also cause problems in the following areas:

- Group Management – If you neglect your emotional intelligence, it will be nearly impossible for you to manage individuals. In order to effectively manage a group, you need to be able to understand relational dynamics and know how to read emotions and behaviors. You need to know if your group members are getting frustrated, if people do not get along, and if there are unresolved issues that are getting in the way. You need to be able to handle emotional conversations confidently and show empathy without getting upset or overwhelmed by your own emotions. There will be times when the group is facing stressful and difficult situations, and you need to have the emotional intelligence to be able to keep a cool head and keep the situation under control.

- Client Relations – If you want to be successful with your clients, you must be able to build good relationships with them. They need to know that you care about them, and that you are willing to work with them to meet their needs. If you cannot read or understand their emotions, you will not be able to connect with them. When a client is angry or upset, you need to be able to allow them to vent and complain without getting triggered or defensive. You need to be able to hear what they are saying, without letting your own emotions or reactions get in the way and prevent you from being able to make good decisions.

- Productivity – Multiple studies have shown that when employees are happy (or at least content), they are more productive. If you do not have strong emotional intelligence, you will not be able to get a good reading on how your employees or coworkers are feeling, and it will be difficult for you to help maintain a positive work environment. Neglecting your emotional intelligence can prevent you from recognizing a problem until it is too late.

Academic Settings

A good education requires more than just skills in reading, writing, and arithmetic. In order to succeed academically you must also have a strong emotional intelligence. If you neglect this aspect, you may encounter some of the following struggles:

- Crippling Anxiety – There is a great deal of stress that students have to deal with. There are deadlines, large workloads, and exams. If you do not have the emotional capacity to deal with these stressors, you can get overwhelmed to the point of shutting down.

You can freeze while taking tests or be unable to accomplish all of your tasks.

- Negative Interactions with Fellow Students – Many courses require group projects as part of the workload. Having low emotional intelligence can make it difficult to work with others, which can make these projects even more cumbersome. You may also find yourself having frequent conflicts with your classmates, or you may struggle to make friends because you are unable to emotionally connect with others.

- Negative Interactions with Educators – There is a lot to be gained from building a strong relationship with your teacher or professor. If you are unable to connect with them, they will not know how to help you. They may also misread you as rude or uninterested. In addition, if you are unable to articulate how you are feeling or whether or not you are struggling, you will not be able to get the help that you need.

- Academic Deficiencies – There are many academic subjects that require a certain amount of understanding of human emotions. Humanities courses, such as history or literature, require you to put yourself in someone else's place and try to understand what they are experiencing. If you cannot do this, you will struggle in these courses.

Now that you are aware of the consequences of not developing your emotional intelligence, let's look at the benefits that come with working hard and enhancing this part of your life.

Benefits of Developing Emotional Intelligence

In addition to avoiding all of the negative consequences, there are numerous benefits to improving your emotional intelligence. Let's take a closer at the ones that are the most impacting.

- Better Understanding of Your Emotions – At the very root of it, you will be able to know how you are feeling and why you are feeling that way. You will not be at the whim of your emotions, but will be able to identify and manage them effectively. You will be able to reach beyond the simple and basic emotions, and start to unpack the complexities of what you are experiencing. As you learn and explore your emotions, you will also learn more about yourself. You will learn what makes you happy as well as what upsets you. You will also find out what angers you and even learn more about your fears. As you dive deeper into these areas, you will also very likely begin to understand more about why you feel the way you do, and can gain a better understanding of yourself, your past, and how it all works together. Facing all of this will undoubtedly help you grow as a person.

- More Resilience – As you learn how to comprehend and regulate your emotions, you will find that you become more resilient. When things do not go your way, you will be better able to bounce back from the disappointment. You will have more courage to try again, and you will realize that you are stronger than you thought you were and able to endure more than you thought was possible. You will start to find that you are more willing to go out on a limb, and that you no longer shrink back from challenges because you know you can handle whatever happens.

- More Empathy – Once you have a better understanding of your own emotions, you will be better able to understand the emotions of those around you. You will find it easier to empathize with others, and you will find that because of this your relationships will flourish. You will also be more aware of the needs around you and will very likely start to work to find a way to meet those needs. This can lead to an increase in your overall happiness, as you will feel positive about helping others.
- Stronger, More Fulfilling Relationships – As you are more connected with your own emotions and the emotions of those around you, your relationships will get stronger. You will find that you begin to trust others more, and they will trust you more. Although you will be more vulnerable, with this vulnerability comes richness and depth of relationships that will truly enhance your life.

Finding a Balance

One thing to keep in mind is that there can be too much of a good thing when it comes to emotional intelligence. As with all things in life, it is important to maintain balance. If you are not careful, there are certain areas where you can start to use emotional intelligence in a negative way. You will need to pay special attention to giving and receiving negative feedback, risk avoidance, and manipulation.

Giving and Receiving Negative Feedback

As your emotional intelligence increases, you may find that it is more difficult for you to give and receive negative feedback. This is due to the fact that you are more aware of and in tune with the emotions of others, and you may hesitate to tell them something that will make them upset. You may want to spare their feelings and could resist being completely honest.

On the other hand, you yourself may become so confident and sure of yourself that you are resistant to negative feedback. This is not because it angers or upsets you, but rather because you do not pay attention to anything that you feel is negative or demeaning. It is essential that you find a balance and remember that there is always room to improve, and that a painful truth is better than a helpful lie.

It is important to remember that when you are giving someone feedback, the most respectful and helpful thing you can do is be honest. You can find ways to be honest without being cruel, and make sure that you are aware of situations that may be difficult for the person you are speaking with. Find a way to deliver the feedback in a gently, but do not lie. Be honest about your intentions and make it clear that, although you have some feedback they may not like, it does not diminish who they are as a person.

When it comes to receiving negative feedback, always take a moment to evaluate your first response. Consider the source of the feedback, then take an honest look to determine if you are rejecting the feedback simply because you do not want to accept it or if there is something that is not trustworthy about the person who is sharing the information with you. Is this a person you respect? Have you asked for the feedback? Is this someone you know loves and cares about you and truly has your best interest at heart? If your answer to these questions is yes, you most likely want to pay attention to what they tell you and assess whether or not there are changes you can make.

Risk Avoidance

As your emotional intelligence increases, so does your awareness of risk. This can potentially cause you to shy away from making daring decisions. You will be more likely to resist being impulsive and will be more self-controlled and make calm and rational decisions. Although this is typically a good quality to have, there are going to be times in your life when it is necessary to take risks. The business world, academics, and even relationships all require some level of risk-taking. Focus on maintaining a balance, and carefully weigh the risk versus the reward in different situations.

As you learn how to navigate different situations, consider asking a trusted friend to help you talk over different situations and opportunities in your life. Ask your friend for honest feedback and advice to help you know if you are being responsible and cautious or if you are possibly missing out on some opportunities for fear of taking a risk.

Manipulation

As you become more aware of your emotions, and more aware of the emotions of others, you will very likely find that you can easily manipulate people. You can empathize with others and know their weaknesses, and then you can use this information against them. It is important to stay balanced and grounded, and not give into the temptation to use your newfound skills to simply get your way. Make sure that you stay aware of the feelings of others and consider how you would feel if someone used and manipulated you.

This is another area where you may find it helpful to have a trusted friend you can talk with. You can ask your friend to check in on you and help remind you of the humanity of everyone you are dealing with.

Review

Here are the top ten things to remember about whether or not it is worth it to increase your emotional intelligence.

1. Neglecting your emotional intelligence can cause problems in your personal relationships. You will have difficulty understanding how your loved ones are feeling and where they are coming from, and you will also have difficulty letting them know how you are feeling.
2. Low levels of emotional intelligence can cause you to unintentionally hurt those you care about. You may be unaware of how they are feeling and say or do something that will cause them additional pain.
3. Those who struggle with emotional intelligence very often struggle in the workplace. Clients want to work with someone who can understand them and meet

their needs, and this is almost impossible to do if you are distant and emotionally unavailable.

4. Poor emotional intelligence can negatively impact you in an academic setting. It can cause you to suffer from severe anxiety and hinder your performance.

5. Humanities studies such as literature and history can be difficult for those with low emotional intelligence. Those subjects require you to consider the perspective and emotions of another person, and if you are unable to accomplish that, you will struggle with the material.

6. Increasing your emotional intelligence will help you have better control over your emotions and prevent you from rising and falling with your feelings.

7. As you gain more awareness of your emotions and how to respond to setbacks and disappointments, you will become much more resilient.

8. One of the most helpful and life-changing effects of increased emotional intelligence is an increase in empathy. As you are better able to understand what those around you are feeling, you will see that your relationships become better, stronger, and more rewarding.

9. As you increase your emotional intelligence, it is important to work on keeping a balanced perspective. This especially applies to the areas of taking risks and giving honest feedback. You need to be willing to take risks when it is appropriate to do so, and you need to be able to tell the truth, even if it is unpleasant.

10. Those with very high levels of emotional intelligence often find that if they so desired, they could easily

manipulate the people around them. As your skills and abilities in this area increase, take care to avoid manipulating others.

Do

After reading this chapter, you have undoubtedly come to the decision that it is worth it. Although right now you may feel confident and eager to get to work, your excitement will inevitably wane a bit over time. As you face more difficult tasks, or when you get tired of working, you will start to find reasons to avoid doing the work. Here are three things you can do now to help you when your motivation lags.

Write It

Look over the material in this chapter and make a list of the top five reasons you are working on improving your emotional intelligence. Although you may have several reasons, for this exercise, limit it to five. Write those five reasons down on an index card and keep that card with you at all times. Put it in your wallet, purse, or backpack. On days when you feel like giving up, read over the card to remember why you are doing this.

You may also want to consider writing yourself an email with a reminder of why you are working on improving your emotional intelligence. Schedule the email to come to you in a week, and again two weeks later, and two weeks after that. Getting the emails in your inbox will help spur you on and can help prevent you from giving up.

Picture It

Find a picture that you associate with high emotional intelligence. It can be something literal, such as a group of people laughing and talking with one another. It can also be something symbolic, such as a picture of a bird to symbolize the freedom that comes with learning to regulate your emotions. Once you have chosen the picture, find a way to look at that picture as often as you can, every day. Consider having the picture as the wallpaper on your phone or computer, or print the picture out and place it in a prominent location. Let this picture serve as a reminder to keep moving forward and making progress.

Tell It

Find someone you trust and tell them what you are working on. Let them know your goals and ask them if they would check in with you on occasion so you can update them on your journey. This will help keep you accountable and can help you move from talking about making a change to actually making a change.

Keep in mind to be selective in who you tell. Although there will be many people in your life who support your journey, there may be some who do not understand what you are trying to do, or who will be intimidated by your goal because they struggle with low emotional intelligence. Choose your confidant wisely, and make sure it is someone who will help motivate you to reach your goal, rather than discourage you.

Now that you have learned that it is worth it to put in the time and effort to increase your emotional intelligence, it is time to get a clear picture of where you stand and what you need to work on. In the next chapter you will learn the warning signs of low emotional intelligence as well as the markers of high emotional intelligence. Be prepared to take a close and honest look at yourself as you determine which areas are your strengths and which areas need some extra attention.

Chapter 5: Where Do I Stand?

"Being entirely honest with oneself is a good exercise."
— Sigmund Freud

Learn

Before you can get started truly making changes and improving your life, it is important to know where you stand and determine your starting point. Let's take a look at warning signs of low emotional intelligence and the indicators of high emotional intelligence. As you read through this material, take an open and honest look at yourself. Don't pass judgment on anything; just make a real and honest assessment. Remember that everyone needs to start somewhere, and the best place to start is to figure out exactly where you are.

Warning Signs of Low Emotional Intelligence

Following is a list of the main warning signs of low emotional intelligence. You will not necessarily exhibit all of the tendencies on this list, and some may be more intense than others. Take time to read over everything, and simply make note of the aspects that stand out to you. Again, it does not need to perfectly describe you, but it may just be a tendency that you have.

- You cannot read other people. Emotional intelligence is what allows you to recognize and understand the emotions other people may be experiencing. If you do not have this ability, you will likely have more conflict with the people in your life. It can often impact you in two different ways. Either you do not recognize the emotions that people are portraying, or you imagine they are portraying something that they are not. For example, you may assume that someone is mad at you and portraying anger, when in reality they are not upset at all. Or, on the other hand, someone may be very upset, and you do not pick up on that fact at all. Do you find yourself frequently surprised by other people's emotional outbursts? Do you feel as if you struggle to understand where other people are coming from? Do you find that you constantly wonder what people are thinking about you, or do you believe people are always angry with you? Can you look around a room and get an idea of what the other people in the room may be feeling? Consider these questions to determine how well you truly read other people.

- You struggle to understand and manage what you are feeling. When you have a high level of emotional intelligence, you are able to sense what you are feeling and experiencing, and you can take steps to calm yourself down before your emotions overtake your behavior. If you feel angry, you can go for a walk or take deep breaths before lashing out. If you are anxious, you can soothe yourself and then focus on the problem at hand. If you do not have a high level of emotional intelligence, you likely find yourself in situations where your anger, anxiety, or sadness have gotten the best of you, and you have acted in a way that you regret. Are you able to understand what you are feeling when you are upset? Do you know why certain things anger you or make you sad? When you get angry, do you have tools you can use to help calm yourself down? On the other end of the spectrum, if you are very excited or happy, are you able to moderate your emotions if you are not in the proper location to freely express what you are feeling?

- You often offend people without realizing you are doing it. If you cannot accurately read or understand the emotions of the people around you, you will most likely have times when you will offend people without realizing you are doing it. While there are people in this world who are very easily offended, if you find that several people around you are hurt or upset by your actions and you don't understand why, you most likely do not have high emotional intelligence. Even if people may not outright tell you that you have offended them, you may notice that people tend to avoid getting into conversations with you or may even cringe or have another physical reaction when speaking with you.

- You have a high level of conflict in several of your relationships. This idea goes hand-in-hand with the idea of offending those around you without realizing you are doing it. If you cannot comprehend the emotions of the people you are interacting with, you are going to see conflict in those relationships. In addition, if you cannot understand or articulate what you are feeling, you will not be able to communicate effectively with your friends and family, and they will not know what you are going through. Although it is

54

normal to have some conflict in relationships, if the majority of your relationships have high amounts of conflict, this could indicate a lack of emotional intelligence.

- You are confused by the emotions of others. This idea goes beyond not understanding what people are feeling. In this situation, you are truly perplexed as to why someone might be upset. You cannot understand why someone would be angry or sad about a certain situation. Their emotional reactions do not make sense to you, and you are unable to put yourself in their position. Again, there may be times when someone has a reaction that is beyond what the situation calls for, but if you frequently find that you are surprised by how people are reacting to someone, it may be a sign of low emotional intelligence.

Indicators of High Emotional Intelligence

Now that you have seen what it looks like to be lacking in emotional intelligence, let's take a quick look at what it is like to have strong emotional intelligence. The following list will not only help you assess where you are but can also give you something to strive for.

- You spend time thinking about feelings. You are aware of your emotions and the emotions of others, and you spend time thinking about them. You watch the way people act and react, and you stop to consider what they might be thinking and feeling and what is driving them do to what they do. You explore what is beyond the surface. You do not only do this with others, but also with yourself. You check in with yourself throughout the day to determine if something is upsetting you or worrying you. You are not afraid to examine what you are thinking and feeling, and you do not judge your emotions. You know what upsets you, what calms you, what makes you angry, and what brings you joy.

- You stop and think before you act. You realize that there are going to be times when your emotions are going to make you want to react. You take time to think things through and consider the possible ramifications before you do anything. You have a series of tools you can use when you are upset that help you regulate your emotions. You know when you need to go for a short walk, take a quick break, or just take a deep breath. There are going to be times that you struggle, as everyone does, but for the most part, you have your behavior under control.

- You take your thoughts under control. You have realized that you are able to control what you think about and where you spend your time and energy. You realize that you do not need to run with every thought you have, and that just because you think something, it does not necessarily mean that it is true. You have learned how to observe your thoughts and are able to analyze them to determine what you should let go, and what you should let take hold.

- You learn from your emotional outbursts. No one is perfect, and there are going to be times when your emotions get the best of you. You have outbursts and meltdowns at times, but after the episode, you try to learn from it. You consider what triggered it and what you can do differently in the future. You do not minimize what happened, but you also do not let it define you. You recognize that it occurred, learn, and move on.

- You are honest, humble, and genuine. You are not afraid to be truthful about who you are. You know your strengths, and you know your weaknesses. You do not pretend to be someone you aren't, and you recognize your faults and work to improve. You also recognize your strengths, and you use them to not only improve your own life, but also the lives around you.

- You have empathy for others. Because you are aware of the feelings of others, you are able to understand what they are going through. You know when they are hurting or angry, and you do what you can to support them. It is not difficult for you to put yourself in someone else's shoes.

- You build up those around you. You encourage people and find ways to strengthen the people in your sphere of influence. You do not feel the need to tear others down, and strong and vibrant people do not intimidate you. You realize that by strengthening those within your circle, you are also strengthening yourself.

- You speak your mind. You are willing to speak the truth, even if it may not be what someone wants to hear. You give your honest opinion on things. You speak out if someone isn't treating you right, and you are able to hold your ground. You have learned how to do this in a calm, assertive way. You are not looking for a fight, but you are also not going to back down.

- You are willing to apologize. You are willing to own up to your mistakes. You apologize, try to make amends, learn from it, and move on. You realize that apologizing does not make you weak or give someone else the upper hand in a relationship. Apologizing is normal, healthy, and a true sign of emotional intelligence and maturity.

- You are true to your word. You do what you say you are going to do, and people know they can rely on you. They know that you will be consistent, and they trust you. Because you have learned to recognize and manage your own emotions, and you know how to meet your own needs, you do not feel the need to lie or cover. You can be honest. You do not over-commit or seek to please people. You know what you can do and you are not afraid to say no.

Review

Here are the top ten things to remember about figuring out where you stand.

1. Be honest. There is no reason to lie about where you are, and there is no shame in admitting what you need to work on. There is also nothing wrong about admitting where your strengths lie. The only way you will improve your emotional intelligence is if you are honest.

2. You will not exhibit all of the traits on either list. Even if you have low emotional intelligence, there are going to be some areas where you struggle more than others. If you have high emotional intelligence, there are always going to be areas you can work on.

3. The inability to get an accurate read on what someone is thinking or feeling is an indicator of low emotional intelligence. You struggle to understand what they are thinking and feeling, and you cannot show empathy.

4. Frequent emotional outbursts are a sign of low emotional intelligence. Because you do not recognize or understand your emotions, you cannot take steps to moderate your behavior in times of upset.

5. If the things you do or say frequently offend the people around you, this could be an indicator that you are deficient in emotional intelligence. One or two people getting offended occasionally may be just a misunderstanding, but if this is something you encounter on a regular basis you need to consider that the problem may be you.

6. High-conflict relationships are often the result of being unable to express your own feelings or understand the feelings of those around you. Good communication is vital to a healthy relationship, and you need to be able to discuss your feelings.

7. In order to have high emotional intelligence, you have to spend time thinking about feelings and emotions.

8. One of the best ways to get your emotions under control is to start taking control over your thoughts. Realize that you do not need to obsess over every thought you have, and that just because you think something, it doesn't necessarily mean that thought is true or correct.

9. An emotionally intelligent person will take the time to build up and encourage others. It takes strength and

confidence to build up people around you without feeling intimidated by them or worried that they will surpass you. The more you practice this skill, the easier it will be.

10. Be honest. Yes, this is a repeat of the first item on this list, but it is absolutely vital. Be honest with yourself. Be honest with others. Let your word be your bond and speak what is on your mind. You will never be able to achieve what you are striving for, or become the person you wish to be, if you do not make truth your standard.

Do

It is time to make the assessment. Complete the following exercises, and then get ready to buckle down and do the hard work.

Look Around

Take a moment to look around at the relationships in your life. Are they strong relationships? Do you have people you can trust, and who trust you? Are your relationships peaceful, or do you have a lot of tension within them? Think of the three closest relationships you have. How would you characterize those relationships? What do you think the other person would have to say? Do you know what he or she is feeling? Do they know what you are feeling? This will give you a bit of an idea of where things stand before you really dive in and look at yourself.

Ask Yourself

Look over the list of warning signs of low emotional intelligence and the indicators of high emotional intelligence. Go through the lists, and mark down which ones resonate with you. Don't judge yourself for them. Just write them down. Simply make a list of your strengths and weaknesses. Remember that you have nothing to be ashamed of, and that this is a huge step toward improving your emotional intelligence.

Ask a Friend

After you have made an honest assessment of yourself, it is time to ask someone else to help you out. Make sure it is someone you trust, and make sure it is someone with whom you have a strong relationship. You may not like what this person will tell you, and you want to make sure your relationship is strong enough to withstand the truth.

Show this person your list of strengths and weaknesses, and ask for honest feedback and if there are any areas you have overlooked. With the help of your friend, craft a final list of what you want to continue doing well, and what you want to work on.

Now that you know where you stand, it is time to get to work. In the next chapter you will learn specific things you can put into practice immediately to start the first step of improving emotional intelligence: Improving the way you manage yourself. You will learn what to watch for, what to strive for, and what practical things you can do right now.

Chapter 6: What Do I Do? Improving Management of Yourself

"You'll never plough a field by turning it over in your mind."
— Irish Proverb

Learn

No matter where you stand, the excellent news is that you can always increase your emotional intelligence. As you work on this skill, there are seven main areas you want to focus on:

- Improving Management of Yourself
- Improving Awareness of Yourself
- Improving Awareness of Others
- Managing Relationships
- Forming Daily Habits
- Mindfulness Practices
- Positive Self-Talk

As we dive into each of these areas, you will find specific things that you can work on. Remember that change is not going to come overnight, and you don't have to tackle everything at once. Take a look at the areas that are of greatest concern to you, choose one or two things to do, and get to work. Once you get used to the changes, add something else. Continue to make one or two small changes at a time, and before you know it, you will notice significant improvement in several areas of your life.

If you try to change everything at one time, you will get overwhelmed. You will not be able to keep up with everything you want to do, and as one thing starts to slip away, you will very likely get discouraged, and before you know it, you will stop moving forward. Small changes are vital, as they add up over time and give you momentum to keep working.

In this chapter we will focus on improving management of you.

What Is Self-Management?

Self-management consists of more than simply keeping yourself in check and your emotional outbursts at bay. It involves taking control of your actions and thoughts and taking responsibility for your behaviors. You realize that although you may not be able to control what is happening around you, you can control how you react to different situations. You do not look to outside forces to help regulate your behavior, but instead you choose to do it for yourself.

Why Does Self-Management Matter?

The simple truth is that you will not be able to make any major changes until you are better able to manage yourself and your emotions. Setting out to improve your emotional intelligence is a good and worthwhile pursuit, but it is not going to be easy. You are going to have to make changes, examine your thoughts, and grapple with difficult realities. None of this will be possible if you cannot manage yourself. No one else can do this for you, and you will not

63

see any lasting change unless you can consistently gain control of yourself.

What Does Self-Management Look Like?

Although self-management can vary depending on your situation in life, there are some basic qualities that apply in all circumstances. These are some of the indicators of a high level of self-management, and things you can strive for:

- Emotional Control – No one goes through life without having things happen that are upsetting. There are setbacks and disappointments everywhere. Self-management allows you to accept these disturbances without losing control of your emotions and having major outbursts. You are able to consider what has just happened and react in a rational and proportionate manner. You are aware of what you are feeling and expressing, and you know how to moderate your behavior. If you feel emotions coming to the surface but are not in a location or setting where it is appropriate to fully express your emotions, you are able to keep them in check until you are free to let go.

- Organization – Organization is a large part of self-management. It allows you to know what you have to do and when you have to do it. You can keep track of your belongings and make sure that you are prepared for whatever comes your way. If you are disorganized and constantly trying to make sense of your surroundings, you will struggle to manage other aspects in your life. You do not have to be completely organized, but you choose to live your life as free of chaos as you possibly can.

- Punctuality – Managing yourself means being able to manage your time. You arrive when you say you will arrive, and you leave when you say you will leave. You realize the value of your time and other people's time, and you make it a priority. You have learned that punctuality lets others know that they can rely on you, and also shows that you have enough discipline and respect to be on time.

- Intentional Living – Self-management does not happen by accident. You have to be intentional about the things that you do. You set goals and standards for yourself, and you work toward those. You don't wander aimlessly through life, but instead, you remain focused on what you are trying to achieve. When you are considering a new opportunity, you stop to determine whether or not this event, change, or action will move you closer to your goals or will somehow get in the way of your goals. If it moves you away from your goals or hinders what you want to do, you have no problem saying no and walking away.

- Reliability – Other people notice when you can manage yourself well. They know they can rely on you to do what you say you are going to do. You begin to build a positive reputation for yourself, both professionally and personally. People recognize and appreciate the fact they can trust you. They see you as mature and confident, and they look to you as a leader, no matter what position you may actually hold.

How Do I Get There?

Work through the following exercises to improve your self-management.

Create a Schedule

In order for you to function at your best, it is important to establish a good sleep routine, get regular exercise, and make healthy food choices. The best way for this to happen is to set a consistent schedule for yourself. You know your time commitments and restraints, and you know what will work best. Don't set a schedule that would work best for someone else—set a schedule that would work best for you. Do you prefer to exercise in the morning? Then wake up earlier so you can do that. Do you have standing appointments in the evening? Then work around those. There is no right or wrong way to make a schedule; the goal is simply to get an established and consistent routine in place. Consider these things as you build your routine:

- Sleep – Make sure that you get enough sleep. You should aim for between 6.5 and 8 hours of sleep every night, but you know what your body needs. Try to go to sleep and wake up around the same time every day, even on weekends. To determine what your body needs, experiment with different amounts of sleep. Eventually you may get to the point where you do not rely on an alarm to wake up in the morning. Your body will get into a rhythm, and you will find that you are operating at your best.

- Exercise – Your body needs daily exercise. This doesn't mean that you need to commit to an intense training regimen unless that is something you want to do. Simply schedule in time for at least thirty minutes of exercise four to five times a week. This can be as simple as a morning or evening walk through the neighborhood. Studies have shown that regular exercise not only helps you physically but also emotionally. Exercise can help reduce your stress, help you sleep better, improve your mood, and increase your self-confidence.

- Meals – Set aside mealtimes every day. Not only will this allow you to take some breaks in your day, but it can also help you become more intentional in what you eat. Aim for a healthy diet, as free from processed foods as possible. Eating at regular intervals can help stabilize your moods, keep you more focused, and give you more energy throughout the day.

- Margin – As you build your schedule, allow for extra time. Perhaps an activity will take longer than you planned, you will have an unexpected visitor, or you may simply just get stuck in traffic. Allowing for this and planning for interruptions can help you handle minor setbacks with as little stress as possible. Do not schedule more activities than you have time for, and also allow time to sit and relax.

Set Goals

What are you hoping to accomplish? Where would you like to see yourself in a year? What changes are you hoping to make in your life? These are all essential questions to ask yourself. Once you have considered these questions, make time to set some goals. They do not have to be extreme or elaborate; they can simply help serve as a guide and reminder for you. They can also help you as you improve your self-management. When you start to get upset or start to react to different situations, stop and ask yourself these two questions:

- Will this action move me closer to my goal or farther away from my goal?
- What can I do in this moment that will help me achieve my goal?

Answer those questions, and then plan your next step accordingly.

Once you have set the goals for yourself, write them down and post them somewhere you will see them regularly. Always keep them in front of you, so you can stay moving forward.

Move to the Music

This exercise will help you realize just how much control you actually have over your body. The more you do this when you are calm and relaxed, the easier it will be to employ these tactics when you are under stress. To begin, turn on some music. Next, choose which part of your body you want to focus on. For example, start by focusing on your hands. As you listen to the music, flex and move your hands to the tempo of the music. Once you have established a good rhythm, change the song. Adjust your movements to the new tempo. Finally, repeat this exercise with different parts of your body. Cycle through your hands, arms, feet, legs, head, and even your shoulders or torso. Not only will this help you better manage yourself, but you will also likely find that it is a fun way to relax.

Learning to control your body movements will help you recognize that you alone hold the power to decide what you will and won't do. This knowledge can help spur you on to controlling other aspects of your life.

Feel It

It is also important for you to understand that you can control your emotions. You can control the things that you think about, and you can help put yourself into situations where you focus on different emotions. Although you may not be able to stop how you feel about a situation or person, you can manage how you express or act on those feelings.

Take some time to let yourself feel different emotions. Begin by choosing to focus on a time when you were truly happy. Don't just simply remember the moment. Think about it in detail. Close your eyes and picture it, and pay attention to the sights and sounds. Remember how you felt. Did you laugh? Did you talk about your feelings? Or did you choose to sit back and simply take it all in? Once you have revisited that memory, focus on the feeling of happiness. Remember what it felt like to be happy and let yourself experience that feeling in the moment.

Once you have focused on happiness, choose a different emotion. Do not be afraid to revisit more difficult emotions, such as sadness, anger, or fear. Remind yourself that you are safe now, and that you are only thinking about the event, but let yourself explore those feelings. Do not shy away from feeling sad, or even regretful, if it applies. After you have let yourself sit in the feeling for a moment or two, bring yourself back to the present. Think about how far you have come or the growth and healing that you have experienced. Even if you are still hurting, take a moment to be thankful that you are taking active steps to learn and grow in your life.

The more you realize that you do not have to be held captive by your emotions, the more you will be able to manage yourself even in difficult times. You will see that although the feelings you have are valid and can be intense, they do not have to dictate your actions.

Review

Here are the top ten things to remember about self-management:

1. Self-management is the most important aspect to work on. Nothing else of consequence can happen without self-management.
2. Self-management allows you to better react to setbacks and disappointments. It helps you realize that although you may not be able to control everything that happens to you, you can control how you react and respond.
3. Emotional control is part of self-management. This means that although you experience a wide range of emotions, you aim to not let those emotions get the best of you and cause outbursts.
4. Organization is another part of self-management. You need to know where things are and know what

you have to do. It is difficult to maintain control of yourself if you feel that everything around you is in chaos.

5. When it comes to self-management, there is no such thing as "fashionably late." Punctuality is a sign that you are able to handle yourself and your responsibilities.

6. Reliability is a byproduct of self-management. Not only will this improve your own life and your career prospects, but it will also have a positive impact on your relationships with other people.

7. A consistent sleep schedule is a vital part of developing self-management skills. You need to be well rested, and getting to bed and waking at the same time every day will help your mind and body function at its peak.

8. Having specific goals can help keep you on track when it comes to regulating your behavior. Before you act, stop to consider if what you are about to do will bring you closer to your goal or push you further away. React accordingly.

9. Remember that you are in control over your body and mind. While there are some things that happen automatically, there is so much that you can control. You can control when and how you move, what you think about, where you focus your time and energy, and what you say.

10. No one is perfect, and there are going to be times when you lose control. When this happens, learn from it. Ask yourself what happened and what you can do differently next time. Make any apologies or amends, and then move on from the incident.

Do

You have been reading, studying, and learning. Now it is time to take action. Do the following things right now:

1. Choose what you are going to do first and set the time you will do it. If you have time to get started right now, then go for it. If not, set a time within the next 24 hours. Getting started is the hardest part, so don't put it off any longer than you have to.
2. Commit to one thing you are going to try to control for the next thirty minutes. This could be as simple as not speaking for a half-hour, working on a project, or even going for a walk. What you choose to do does not matter. The point is to make a decision and do it. Immediately.
3. Find at least one thing to celebrate in this moment. For example, you finished reading this chapter. That is an accomplishment, so take time to acknowledge it. Think of some other things that you have done today. Maybe you had a healthy breakfast or you avoided an argument with a coworker. Whatever you think of, realize that in that moment you showed self-management. Realize that you are on your way and keep moving forward.

Now that you understand more about managing yourself and are working on correctly managing your emotions as they come to the surface, it is time to get more insight into what exactly you are feeling. In the next chapter we will focus on improving awareness of yourself. Not only will this help you identify what you are feeling at any particular moment, but it will also help you understand what you might potentially feel and think about a situation. You will be better prepared for difficult situations and also better able to voice what you need.

Chapter 7: What Do I Do? Improving Awareness of Yourself

"To know yourself, you must sacrifice the illusion that you already do."
— *Vironika Tugaleva*

Learn

Once you have learned to manage yourself and have better control over what you say and do, you will be able to start really exploring how you feel and become better aware of yourself.

What Is Self-Awareness?

Having self-awareness means being connected to your emotions and knowing what is going on in your mind. You know if you are feeling angry, sad, excited, or tired. You know how your past experiences have shaped you, and you understand what could upset you or cause problems for you. You know when you need to take time away from a situation, and you know when there is something bothering you that is causing you to react or respond differently than you normally would.

Why Does Self-Awareness Matter?

Self-awareness matters because if you are unaware of your own emotions, you will not be aware of anyone else's emotions. In order to have emotional intelligence, you must be able to stop and consider what is going on inside your own mind. You will gain a better understanding of yourself, and you will also know how you see the world and what preconceived ideas you may have. This will impact all areas of your life, including your relationships with other people.

What Does Self-Awareness Look Like?

Following is a list of common traits you will find in someone who is highly self-aware:

- A self-aware person will spend more time listening than talking. Someone who knows who they are, what they think, and how they feel does not feel the need to talk all the time. When they are having a conversation with someone, they will actually listen to what the other person has to say.

- Self-aware people spend time examining their own thoughts. They know what they are thinking, and they strive to understand what is causing those thoughts. They are not afraid to look for errors in their thinking or judgment, and they will make changes as necessary.

- A self-aware person is not afraid of receiving feedback and will actually welcome constructive criticism. He or she know that there is always something to work on and appreciates the opportunity to learn and grow.

- Self-aware people know what will trigger or upset them. They will approach certain situations with caution and will give themselves time to process through any negative emotions that might arise. They do not shy away from difficult or challenging situations; they simply know what to expect and know how to handle it.

- A self-aware person is able to articulate what he or she needs without feeling guilty. Being self-aware means knowing your weaknesses and your strengths, and being willing to advocate for yourself so you can be at your very best.
- A self-aware person accepts what he or she is thinking or feeling without judgment. This allows the person to be honest and recognize when there are issues that need to be addressed without falling into a spiral of guilt and shame.

How Do I Get there?

The following exercises will help you improve your self-awareness.

Write It Out

Write down the things you are thinking and feeling. However, do this in two different ways. Do it once without thinking, and then again while thinking. Keep two separate notebooks for each activity. Label one as your stream of consciousness journal, and one as your everyday journal.

- Stream of Consciousness Journal – Every day, as soon as you wake up, write in this journal for at least five minutes. Write down whatever comes to mind. Do not stop to censor it, and do not pass judgment on anything. Write it down, and get it out of your head and on to paper. When you are finished, read it over. This will help you see what is at the forefront of your mind and will give you an idea of what you need to focus on or work on for the day. There are no right or wrong things to write down – just write whatever comes to mind, as it comes to mind. The more you practice this, the easier it will get.

- Everyday Journal – Use this journal to keep track of the things that you are going through on a day-to-day basis. Record your thoughts and feelings, struggles you are facing, and how you are working through those struggles. Record the good and the bad that happens, and use this journal to keep a record of your life. Periodically read back through your journal. This will not only help you be more aware of your thoughts and emotions, but will also help you see just how far you have come.

Test It Out

Although a personality test cannot tell you everything you need to know, it can give you some insight and can also help you take a closer look at yourself. Set aside time to take some personality tests. There are a wide range of tests available online, ranging from the more serious tests such as established personality profiles or workplace productivity tests to more frivolous tests such as which movie or television character you identify with. Remember that the point of this exercise is not to get an official assessment, but rather for you to become more aware of who you are. You will find that as you take these tests, you start to examine yourself more. You will think about what you like and don't like and how you operate. You will likely be asked to consider how you respond to different situations and circumstances.

As these questions come up, stop to take note of what you are learning about yourself. Remember that the test is simply a tool to help you be more aware of yourself. Let the questions get you thinking, and then follow where your thoughts go.

Talk It Out

As you work to improve your emotional intelligence, you may want to seriously consider finding a therapist. A licensed therapist can help you discover who you really are. A therapist knows the questions to ask and can give you valuable tools that you can use as you move forward.

Review

These are the top ten things to remember about improving awareness of yourself.

1. Be patient with yourself. Remember that this process is going to take time, so give yourself the time that you need. You may feel frustrated that you are not progressing faster, but be aware of the fact that you are making major changes to your life. The small changes will add up over time, and before you know it, you will see growth.

2. Do not judge your thoughts or emotions, but instead, simply acknowledge them. If you start to judge yourself for what you are feeling, you will be very tempted to stop being honest about it. You will want to avoid anything that you think is negative, and you will be less aware of what is truly going on inside of your mind. Work to get to the point where you truly believe that whatever you think and feel is okay. You do not need to apologize for your feelings, and you do not need to explain them to anyone, including yourself. Accept what you feel and learn from it.

3. There are countless emotions, and you will experience several of them at one time. Being self-aware means being able to recognize how you are feeling and to know that it is possible to be sad about one situation while at the same time feeling excited and hopeful about another.

4. Being self-aware means having an acceptance of who you are and getting to a point of being comfortable with it. You may notice things that you would like to change, but you will give yourself the time and space that you need to make those changes.

5. In order to truly be self-aware, you need to commit some time to examining your thoughts. Again, do not pass judgment on your thoughts. Simply acknowledge them and try to gain an understanding of why you feel the way you do.

6. Self-aware people are not afraid of feedback. They realize that they are continually learning and growing, and feedback will help them along the way. Self-aware people even seek out feedback from trusted sources knowing that it will help them become stronger people.

7. A self-aware person is not afraid to speak up and advocate for himself or herself. He or she has put in the work to learn what they need and will ask for it without guilt. He or she also knows how to say, "No," and will do so without regret or apology.

8. Journaling is an excellent way to become more aware of your thoughts and feelings. Remember not to edit yourself as you go. Write down what you are thinking, and be honest. The journal is for your eyes

only, and being honest with yourself is the only way you will truly gain an understanding of who you are.

9. Even seemingly silly personality tests can help you become more self-aware. Although it may not be much in the grand scheme of life, knowing what your favorite dessert says about you can help open your eyes to part of your personality, and help you be a stronger person in the long run.

10. Consider finding a qualified therapist to help you on your journey of discovering who you are, what you think, and how you feel. A therapist has been trained on how to help you understand yourself more, and can also give you valuable tools for emotional intelligence. Know that there is no shame in seeking professional help. It is wise to use whatever resources you may have at your disposal.

Do

Although there are several action steps you can take right now, these three are the most important:

1. Verbally acknowledge the importance of taking time to become more self-aware. You can do this by just saying the words out loud to yourself, or you can say them to a trusted friend. Speaking the words will help solidify it in your mind and will make you more likely to follow-through on other actions.

2. Get a journal. No matter what style of journaling you choose to do, get started. Get the thoughts out of your head and down on to paper. Although this may seem like a simple idea, realize that it is a big step to take, and reward yourself for taking it.

3. Commit to not judging your thoughts or feelings, and create little reminders not to judge yourself. This can be as simple as a note on your phone or mirror. Remember, the minute you start passing judgment on yourself, the more likely you are to stop being honest and become less self-aware.

Now that you are more aware of yourself and managing yourself, it is time to turn your attention outward. You do not live in a vacuum, so in order to successfully navigate through life, you have to be aware of those around you. This means not only knowing and acknowledging what they tell you, but also learning to read the subtle signs that there is more going on under the surface. In the next chapter you will learn more about improving your awareness of others.

Chapter 8: What Do I Do? Improving Awareness of Others

"I do believe that in order to be a successful negotiator that as a diplomat, you have to be able to put yourself into the other person's shoes. Unless you can understand what is motivating them, you are never going to be able to figure out how to solve a particular problem."
— *Madeleine Albright*

Learn

Since you do not live on a deserted island, it is essential that you are aware of others. You must learn to read their body language, watch their actions, listen to what they are saying, and really try to understand what they are thinking and feeling. This will improve your emotional intelligence, but it will also vastly improve your relationships.

What is Awareness of Others?

Awareness of others means recognizing the people around you and working to understand what they are going through. It is more than just acknowledging that they have thoughts and feelings; it includes a curiosity or desire to know why they are experiencing certain emotions. Even though you may think you know what someone is feeling, or you know how you would feel in a specific situation, you do not assume that the person you are talking with feels that way. You take the time to ask them how they feel, and you truly try to understand what they are going through.

Awareness of others also includes the desire to ask questions and really listen to other people as they share their stories and experiences. It involves learning as much as possible about the people around you and putting in the effort to connect. When you talk to someone, you do not simply wait for your chance to speak. You pay attention, listen, and ask questions if something is unclear to you or if you want to learn more.

Why Does Awareness of Others Matter?

A key aspect of emotional intelligence is being able to read the people around you. Not only does this let you know how they are doing, but also it helps you know what is and is not appropriate in different situations. Being aware of other people helps strengthen your relationships, helps you develop empathy, and makes you a stronger person.

What Does Awareness of Others Look Like?

People who are keenly aware of others exhibit many, if not all, of the following traits:

- They listen. It is impossible to know and understand what others are thinking and feeling if you do not listen. Being aware of other people means truly hearing them when they talk and paying attention to what they say. It is being engaged during conversation, and not just waiting for your turn to speak.
- They ask questions. The best way to get to know someone is to ask questions, and don't settle for simple answers. Ask follow-up questions. If someone tells you they are having a rough day, ask them what

is going on or how you can best support them. If someone tells you they are excited, find out what they are looking forward to. People who are aware of others know that oftentimes people don't want to share too much information upfront, but are more than willing to open up if they are asked just a few simple questions.

- They repeat what they hear. This doesn't mean that they repeat what they hear to other people. That is gossip and is not an indicator of emotional intelligence. They repeat what they hear to the person who is talking to them. They don't simply assume they know what the other person is feeling, but instead they clarify. They say things such as "What I hear you saying is…" or "Is this what you mean?" This helps clear up confusion.

- They pay attention to body language. Being aware of other people means realizing that they often do not express what they are really thinking or feeling. Paying attention to body language will help you know if someone is upset, uncomfortable, shy, or even afraid.

- They are thoughtful. They pay attention to what is going on around them and will stop to consider how others may be affected. They realize that just because something doesn't upset or bother them, it doesn't mean that it might not be difficult for someone else. They are able to think beyond themselves and their own experiences.

How Do I Get There?

The following exercises will help you improve your awareness of others.

Sit and Watch

Set aside some time to just go and watch people for a while. Although this may seem strange at first, it is an excellent way to start noticing others and pick up on social cues and even subtle gestures that happen during different interactions.

Go to a park, a mall, or a busy restaurant and just sit back and watch. Watch facial expressions, watch the way people walk together, and watch the way people stand and talk with one another. As you are watching, try to piece together what may be happening in front of you. Is there a couple that is arguing? Is there a mom growing impatient with her children? Are there two friends getting reacquainted after a long absence?

Although you will most likely never know for sure what is happening and will not get a definitive answer, this practice will increase your awareness of others and help you develop the habit of trying to consider what others may be going through.

Take Notice

Once you have spent some time watching people from a distance, start taking note of the number of people you interact with on a daily basis. Think beyond just those in your immediate circle and start to consider people with whom you may just have a passing interaction. It could be a barista at a coffee shop, a salesclerk at a store, or even a crossing guard on your daily commute.

Once you are aware of these people, pay a bit of attention to them. You don't need to pry into their personal lives, but consider their demeanors. Do they seem happy? Are they tired? Does it seem as if they are having a tough day? You don't need to get answers to these questions— simply spend a little bit of time thinking about them and noticing what is in front of you.

Turn the Sound Off
Studies have shown that anywhere between 70% and 90% of communication is nonverbal. In order to effectively improve your awareness of others, you need to be able to pick up on non-verbal cues. For this exercise, choose a movie or television show that you are familiar with. Start watching, but turn off the sound. Pay attention to the character's faces, body movements, and other non-verbal cues. Remember that these are paid actors who typically know how to communicate nonverbally, so this is a good way to learn, as what they are doing is most likely intentional. Watching their movements can help you know what to look for when you are interacting with people in real life.

Only Hear the Sound
For this activity, you are going to do the exact opposite of what you did in the previous activity. Choose a show where people will be discussing their feelings. This can be a reality show, a daytime talk show, or even a televised courtroom show. The subject matter is not really important; it just needs to be something where people will be expressing emotions.

Once you have chosen the show, listen to it. Do not watch it—simply listen. Listen to what they are saying. Pay attention to the words that indicate their feelings. Listen to the tone of voice they are using. Can you pick out anger? Do you recognize sarcasm? Perhaps there is excitement or fear?

Doing this activity a few times a week will help you become more aware of other people and the way they express their emotions.

Clarify

The best way to understand what someone is thinking and feeling is to ask them directly. Rather than assume what they are going through, ask them. If you think they may be upset, find out what is going on. Get comfortable asking these questions:

- What is on your mind?
- Are you upset about something?
- I hear you saying you are angry (sad, scared, etc.). Is this correct?

Doing this will not only help you have a better understanding of the other person, but will also help them see that you are truly interested in what they are going through.

Read

One of the best ways to become more aware of others is to read about people who have a different life than you do. You do not necessarily have to read entire biographies, although if you have the time to do so, you may really enjoy it. You can learn a lot about other people by simply reading articles online. Look up different types of people and learn about them. Learn about people from other races and economic brackets. Learn the struggles they face, the accomplishments they have enjoyed, and a bit about their history. Learn about people in other cultures. Learn how they interact and communicate, what forms of emotional expression are accepted, and what are frowned upon. Learn as much as you can about as many different people as you can. As you do this, you will most likely discover that you are better connected to people around you because you have learned to study people in general.

Body Language Primer

Body language is such a vital part of communication, and if you are able to improve your ability to read body language, you will undoubtedly improve your awareness of others. Take time to learn these most common body language indicators:

- Crossed arms – if someone is talking to you and they have their arms crossed in front of their chest, they are most likely trying to protect or defend themselves from what they are hearing. They may disagree with what is being said and they may be angry. They are closing themselves off from the words, as well as from the person speaking the words. Tread lightly if you see someone doing this. Do not draw attention to it, but consider changing the subject to something that is neutral or asking them a question about what they enjoy doing. This will help them relax, as they will realize that you are not there to be their enemy, but that you truly want to engage and connect with them.

- Biting nails – People typically bite their nails when they are anxious, worried, or stressed. It can also be a sign that they are feeling insecure. There are some people who have just developed a habit of biting their nails, but this action typically indicates that someone is in distress. If you see someone doing this, do not point it out. It is likely a deeply ingrained habit, and if you call attention to it, you can make them feel embarrassed and even more anxious. Simply talk with them and give them a chance to share what they are thinking or feeling. They will probably enjoy having someone with whom they can share their worries or fears, or they may be shy and insecure, and having the chance to talk with someone can help them feel more comfortable.

- Head tilted – If you are speaking with someone and their head is tilted to the side, this is an indication that they are really listening to you and paying attention to the things that you are saying. Know that they are truly interested in you and be confident that they want to continue the conversation.

- Palms facing upward – If someone is talking to you and their hands are outward with their palms facing up, this is a sign that they are being open and honest. They may also be a bit submissive, or letting you know that they are innocent.

- Straight posture – This is an indicator of confidence and self-assuredness. Someone who is walking, sitting, or standing with their back straight and shoulders back most likely knows who they are and feels secure. They are not intimidated and feel as if they are on equal footing with whomever they are speaking with. If you are speaking with someone who is standing this way, know that they are comfortable and feel in control of the situation. Focus on holding your posture in the same way to exude confidence. If you are walking into a situation where you feel uncomfortable, or if you have to speak with someone who has authority over you, work on holding your posture straight as you enter the conversation. This will send the message that you are not intimidated.

- Eye contact – If someone makes regular eye contact without looking away suddenly, they are very likely confident and trustworthy. However, too much prolonged eye contact can mean that they are hiding something or lying. Prolonged, unwavering eye contact can also mean that someone is trying to be intimidating. If someone avoids eye contact completely, it means that they are trying to hide something. They may be uncomfortable and unwilling to share, or they may be lying. Be aware that it can be difficult to get a true reading on someone based on eye contact alone, as most people are aware that eye contact is an easily detectible form of non-verbal communication. For example, experienced liars have learned how to maintain just enough eye contact so no one suspects them of lying without being too obvious. When you are assessing a situation and paying attention to body language, make note of eye contact, but also compare it with the other nonverbal cues you are receiving.

- Fidgeting – Constant fidgeting can be a sign that someone is nervous or insecure. They may be actively trying not to cross their arms, but they are still trying to shield themselves and pull away from the situation. It can also be a sign that they are bored. If you are in a conversation with someone and they are fidgeting, try and steer the conversation to a subject that you know will be enjoyable for them, or something they will find interesting. Even if someone is shy or insecure, they will likely be more able to relax when talking about themselves and things that make them happy. Ask about their hobbies or their favorite books or music. Find ways to draw them into conversation without feeling put on the spot or feeling that they will be judged.

Review

These are the top ten things to remember about improving awareness of others.

1. Awareness of others is essential if you want to have high emotional intelligence. You do not exist in a vacuum, so it does not matter how well you know yourself and how well you know your own emotions. If you cannot recognize the people around you, know how they are feeling, pay attention to them, and empathize, you do not have strong emotional intelligence.

2. The more you notice the people around you, the more you will notice the wide range of emotions that are expressed without words. You will also notice that people will often express one feeling or emotion

with words and another with their body. When this happens, listen to the nonverbal communication. People can choose their words and will often try and hide what they are feeling, but body language and nonverbal cues are more difficult to fake.

3. One of the best ways to increase your awareness of others is to listen for the sake of listening. Although it can be tempting to listen with the intent of forming your response or what you would like to say, this will not help you understand the other person. Work on simply listening to what they are telling you. Take note of the information and realize that they are opening up and sharing a part of their life with you.

4. As you are talking with people, ask questions. Ask questions that require more than just a yes or no answer, listen to the response, and then ask follow-up questions. If you sense that a person does not want to talk about a subject, do not pry. However, do not end the conversation there, either. Simply ask another question and find a subject that is less troublesome.

5. Once you think you understand what the other person is saying, take a moment to clarify. Repeat what you think they are trying to say, just to make sure you are hearing them correctly. Much conflict can be avoided if each person in the conversation or relationship makes an effort to clarify misunderstandings before getting upset.

6. Pay attention to body language. There is so much that a person says without uttering a word. To truly be aware of others, you have to be able to read body language.

7. Sitting and watching people is an excellent way to improve your awareness of others. You will notice things that you never really paid attention to. You will be able to tell when people are truly engaged in a conversation or when one person has checked out. Once you have spent time examining other conversations, you will be able to notice these tendencies when you are interacting with people.

8. Although there are different types of body language, the main idea is that if someone is doing something to hide or block themselves, then they are not comfortable. If their body is relaxed and open, then they are most likely at ease. People instinctively move away from things they don't like, so if you sense that someone is trying to move away from a group or conversation, it is very likely they are uncomfortable.

9. Prolonged and unwavering eye contact is a sign that someone is very likely being dishonest. It typically indicates they are trying too hard to appear truthful. If someone is honest, he or she will usually maintain eye contact for some time, but then look away for a moment or two before making eye contact again.

10. Being more aware of others will also increase your awareness of yourself. As you see different emotions expressed and different tendencies that people may have, you may start to realize that you do the same things.

Do

The most important thing that you can do right now is set up a reminder to focus on other people. There are a wide variety of things that you can do, but it is important to choose something that will be meaningful to you and will cause you to stop and be aware of others. You can set a reminder on your phone, write a note and stick it on your mirror, wear something on your wrist, or set it as the wallpaper on your computer. Whatever you choose to do, let it help spur you into taking active steps toward increasing your awareness of others and improving your emotional intelligence.

Another excellent step that you can do immediately is just commit to spending at least ten minutes a day truly engaging with another person. This can be a conversation over lunch or dinner, time with your family, or even just going for a short walk with a friend. Setting aside time to connect with another person will help you realize the value of making time for others, and you will most likely want to continue doing this in other areas of your life.

Yet another component of emotional intelligence is the ability to manage and navigate relationships. Relationships can be difficult, no matter what the context. Both people in the relationship have their own thoughts and feelings, want to be heard and understood, and need to feel appreciated. The next chapter will focus on managing relationships, giving you key insight and specific actions to take.

Chapter 9: What Do I Do? Managing Relationships

"If civilization is to survive, we must cultivate the science of human relationships—the ability of all peoples, of all kinds, to live together, in the same world at peace."
— Franklin D. Roosevelt

Learn

As you improve your self-management, self-awareness, and awareness of others, your relationships will start to improve. You will be better able to understand what you are thinking and feeling and be able to express that. You will also be better able to understand the other person and be able to pick up on what they are feeling. However, good relationships do not happen by accident. If you want to have strong and healthy relationships, you have to work at them.

What Does It Mean to Manage Relationships?

Managing relationships involves moving beyond merely knowing what the other person is thinking and feeling, and instead, it is using that information to develop stronger and healthier relationships. It is a two-way street, as it involves both people in the relationship to interact, be vulnerable at times, and trust one another. It means learning how to handle conflict in such a way that the relationship is ultimately stronger. It means finding a balance between giving and receiving, and being able to work through difficulties together so that both people in the relationship are satisfied.

Why Is Managing Relationships Important?

Unless you want to go through your entire life alone, you must learn to manage relationships. Doing so will help increase your emotional intelligence, improve your satisfaction levels, and can give you a richer and more fulfilling life.

Imagine how peaceful and fulfilling a relationship would be if both people were committed to demonstrating emotional intelligence. If both people were willing to understand and regulate their own emotions, and were willing to truly try to understand the other person in the relationship, there would be much more peace. There would still be conflict, because everyone has their own thoughts and opinions, and these do not always line up with those of someone else, but even when there is conflict, there can be better and more open ways of resolving the conflict when both people are committed to managing the relationship.

Studies have shown that there are many additional benefits of developing and maintaining strong and healthy relationships. These benefits include:

- Having less stress. Studies have found that when someone is in a healthy relationship, they produce less stress hormones than someone who is not in a relationship. If you have relationships with people and you do face stressful and difficult times, you know that you are not alone. You have people you can go to who can help carry the load, which will reduce the amount of stress that you personally feel. Oftentimes, just being able to talk with someone about how you feel will help you release stress.

- Having a healthier lifestyle. It can be a lot easier to commit to a healthy lifestyle if you have someone doing it with you. Having strong relationships with friends, romantic partners, families, or even teammates or coworkers can give you more opportunities to get out and be active. You can plan to take hikes or bike rides together, try a new sport together, or attempt other adventures such as kayaking or rock climbing. You can try out healthy recipes together or just commit to eating less sugar. It does not matter how big or small of change you want to make; having healthy relationships and people to make those changes with you will make it easier, and will make a difference.

- Healing better. Numerous studies have shown that when someone has had a major injury, illness, or surgery, they have a much easier recovery when they have someone to help them through the process. This can be as extensive as having someone to help give you medication and change bandages, or as simple as having someone call and check on you to see how you are feeling or stop by with a bunch of flowers. Cultivating and maintaining positive relationships not only helps your emotional health, but your physical health as well.

- Having a sense of value and purpose in life. When you have a relationship with someone, you realize that your actions and attitudes matter. Your behaviors affect someone other than yourself. As you realize this, and when you realize that you make a difference, you will find a greater purpose in your life.

- Living longer. With all of the benefits listed above, you can see how it is possible that healthy relationships can help you live longer. You have less stress, and less of the negative health effects that come from stress. You can be more active and live a healthier lifestyle, which can add years to your life. And finally, you have a sense of purpose and meaning, and will most likely make better and more responsible choices because you know that your life has an impact on those around you.

What Does Managing Relationships Look Like?

Every relationship is different, but there are certain indicators that you are managing a relationship well. For example, you regularly set aside time to check in with the other person and make sure that he or she is content with the way things are going. Also, you are willing to have difficult conversations, and you don't avoid conflict. Finally, you make it a priority to spend time with the other person.

How Do I Get There?

The very fact that you are aware of and working on improving your relationships will make a difference, but there are other things that you can do as well. Try the following activities to help better manage your relationships.

Nothing But Each Other

Set aside time at least once a week to interact with this person where you have nothing else around you but each other. This can apply to a romantic partner, a business associate, a friend, or a child. The amount of time can vary depending on the type of relationship you have with the person, but the point is to have no other distractions. No phones and no television; just you and the person you are interacting with. Ask questions, tell stories, or even point out absurdities you see around you. Don't use this time to try and resolve conflict. It is a time just to connect, even if it is only for a few minutes.

Have Fun

Make time to have fun together. Watch a movie, go for a walk, play a game together, or do something else that you both would enjoy. Life is full of stress and difficult situations, so it is important to carve out time to just relax and have a good time.

Look for the Good

It is easy to see the negative aspects of another person. They are going to do and say things that annoy you. While it is important to address major concerns, it is also important to find the things that you appreciate and then let them know. Make it a point to look for the good. Say thank you for little things, such as holding a door open, handing you a pencil, or bringing you a cup of water. If something good happens for them, acknowledge it. Celebrate successes, and let this person know that you want good things for them.

Apologize

This is not an easy one, but it is essential if you want to have good relationships. No one likes to admit they are wrong, and it can be uncomfortable to be vulnerable and apologize. It is also one of the best ways to strengthen your relationships, as it shows that you know you aren't perfect, and that you are willing to admit when you have made a mistake. It helps resolve conflict, and also lets the other person in the relationship know that they do not have to strive for perfection either. It encourages openness and honesty, and it allows minor setbacks to actually bring you closer together.

Review

These are the top ten things to remember about managing relationships.

1. Learning to manage relationships will not only help you have greater emotional intelligence, but it will also strengthen your connections with people and help you have a more fulfilling life.
2. Good, strong relationships do not happen by accident. You have to be intentional about making the relationship a priority.
3. In addition to helping improve your emotional intelligence, managing relationships well can also help improve your health.
4. Studies have shown that those who are in healthy relationships have lower stress levels than those who are not. They actually produce less of the stress hormone cortisol.
5. Managing relationships can also help you have less stress by giving you someone to help carry the load. You will have someone to talk to and you will realize that you are not alone.
6. As you spend more time focusing on improving and managing your relationships, you will very likely notice that you start to have a healthier lifestyle. You

will likely get out and do things more and become more active.

7. Another benefit of learning to manage relationships better is that you will be more content with your life and will feel a greater sense of purpose.

8. As you work on improving your relationships, it is important to make sure that you set aside time to have some fun. You will have important discussions, but there are also going to be times when you need to just relax and cut loose a bit.

9. It is important to make time to intentionally seek out the good in the people in your life and acknowledge it. It can be very easy to get stuck in a pattern of negativity. Although you do need to recognize and work on the negative aspects of relationships, take time to stop and appreciate that which is positive.

10. Do not be afraid to apologize. Apologizing will strengthen your relationships, will increase your strength and emotional intelligence, and can help facilitate healing for those whom you may have wronged. It can be a bit intimidating to be vulnerable and apologize, but it is worth it.

Do

The best way to begin managing your relationships better is to be intentional about spending time with the people in your life. Begin by making a list of the five most important relationships in your life. Set aside time this week to connect with all five of the people on your list. It can be as simple as sending a text message to check in, or making a quick phone call. If you have more time, consider getting together for lunch, going for a walk together, or finding another fun way just to spend time together.

As you have learned about managing and being more aware of yourself, improving your awareness of others and better managing your relationships, you may be starting to feel overwhelmed and wonder how you can do everything. Don't get discouraged. The next chapter will discuss how to form daily habits that will help you improve your emotional intelligence. This will help you see that as you start to make small but intentional changes, it will become easier to implement the things you have learned.

Chapter 10: What Do I Do? Forming Daily Habits

"Depending on what they are, our habits will either make us or break us. We become what we repeatedly do."
— Sean Covey

Learn

If you truly want to increase your emotional intelligence, it needs to become a lifestyle. You need to implement daily habits that will keep your mind moving in the right direction. If you do not actively work against it, you will fall back into your old way of life. Once you learn how to form a new habit, focus on implementing the following practices into your daily routine:

- Gratitude
- Meditation
- Focus on others
- Downtime

What Does It Mean to Form a Habit?

A habit is something that you do regularly and predictably. You very likely do not even think about the habit before you do it. It has become part of your normal routine, and it is something you are consistent about. A habit does not form overnight. It takes intentional and consistent work.

Why Are Habits Important?

Habits are important because as your brain becomes accustomed to the behavior, it creates pathways, and you actually begin to crave the reward that comes from the behavior. It does not necessarily need to be a big reward. For example, it could be the reward of feeling good after exercising, the satisfaction of seeing a clean house, or simply the knowledge that you have made healthy food choices. Once your brain starts to crave the reward, it is easier to do the behavior. Additionally, once a behavior becomes a habit, you no longer need to think about it or have to make a decision as to whether or not you are going to do it. It becomes automatic and frees your mind up to handle other more important matters.

What Does Having Habits Look Like?

There are specific ways to determine that something has become a habit, rather than just something that you do on occasion or even frequently. Following is a list of specific ways to know that a behavior has become a habit:

- It is consistent. In order for something to be a habit, you have to do it regularly. It does not necessarily mean that you have to do it every day, but it has to be done on a very regular and consistent basis. For instance, cleaning the bathroom twice a week could become a habit. If you make it a point to clean the bathroom every Tuesday and Saturday at 7:00 AM, and you regularly and consistently do this, it can become a habit. A habit could also be getting up at the same time every day.

- It does not require will power. When something has become a habit for you, you don't even think twice before doing it. You don't have to convince yourself that it is worth it, and you don't try to find reasons not to do it. You just do it. For example, for most people, putting on a seatbelt is a habit. The minute you get into a car, you put on your seatbelt without thinking. This is a habit. You don't have to motivate yourself or give yourself a reward afterward. You just do it. However, for many people, exercising is not a habit. You have to force yourself to do it. You have to use willpower to get yourself to the gym or go out for a walk. It is something that you need to think about, and it does not come naturally or easy to you, because it is not yet a habit. However, once exercising does become a habit, you will not need willpower to do it.

- If you forget to do it, it seems like something is missing or something is wrong. To continue with the example of the seatbelt, when you get into a car and don't fasten your seatbelt, you feel as if you are forgetting something. Or if you have a habit of locking your front door whenever you leave the house, if for some reason you get distracted one day and don't do it, or you have something in your hands and can't lock the door, you notice it. Something is missing.

- You do it without realizing what is happening. Until a few minutes ago, you probably did not ever think about the fact that you put on your seatbelt every time you get in the car. It is a natural, fluid motion that you do without thinking. That is because it is a habit.

How Do I Get There?

It takes time to form a new habit. There is no set amount of time, but research has shown that it takes on average a little over two months to have a habit set in stone. This means that some habits will form more quickly, but some can take up to eight months. Here are some strategies to help you form a new habit.

- Choose one habit at a time. Although you may want to change everything at once, this is not the best strategy. You will most likely get overwhelmed quickly, give up, and not make any changes at all. Choose one thing at a time and focus your attention on that one aspect of your life.
- Make a commitment to stay with it for as long as it takes, but plan at least sixty days. Clear time on your calendar and make the new habit a priority. You will need to be intentional about doing it every day, even when you don't want to.
- Connect your new habit to a habit you already have. For example, if you want to commit to journaling every morning, attach that time to a habit that is already in place. If you drink coffee every morning, commit to spending time journaling while you drink your first cup. You already have the habit of the coffee so adding in one more thing will not be too big of a change.
- Start small. Break your ultimate goal into smaller steps, and make small changes at a time. For example,

if you want to eventually journal for at least thirty minutes a day, start by committing to five minutes a day. Once you have completed two weeks of five minutes a day, bump the time up to ten minutes. Then go to fifteen. Continue to increase by small increments until you reach your goal.

- Plan ahead for when you want to give up. Although you may have a lot of energy and excitement right now, this will wane. There are going to be days when you want to give up. You will try and justify taking a break from the habit or relaxing your commitment a bit. Do not give in to this temptation, and do not get caught off guard by it. Plan ahead for this. Set in stone that you will push through no matter what. Ask a friend to hold you accountable, make a list to remind you of why you want to establish this new habit, or simply set a reward for yourself that you cannot have until you have finished the task for the day. Remember that the feeling will pass, and you will ultimately be grateful that you stuck with your plan.

- Celebrate milestones. Take time to notice when you have stuck with your habit for a week, two weeks, a month, and other times. Mark the occasion by doing something special for yourself. It can be as simple as taking a leisurely walk or spending time reading your favorite book. For bigger milestones, choose bigger celebrations.

- Once the habit is set, keep it a priority even as you introduce a new habit to your routine. It is important that you not lose sight of this change as you begin to make other changes. It will not take as much time or energy, but simply check in to make sure you are doing all of the things you want to do.

Gratitude

One of the best and most important habits you can form is setting aside time every day to practice gratitude. No matter what is going on in your life or how bleak things may seem, there are things for which you can be grateful. Intentionally focusing on these things can help change your overall outlook on life. It will improve your emotional intelligence as well as your overall mental health. Try the following exercises to help you focus on gratitude.

Fill the Jar

Choose a jar, or a box, or some sort of container. If you are so inclined, decorate the container to help set it apart. Place the container where you will see it every day and place a stack of paper or sticky notes and a pen next to the container. Throughout the day, write down things you are thankful for on a piece of paper, and then put the paper in the jar. You can be thankful for little things such as a cup of coffee, butter on your toast, or fuzzy socks. You can also be thankful for bigger things such as money in the bank, friends and family, or your health. There is nothing too little or too big to write on the slips of paper. Commit to adding to the jar at least three times a day. When the jar is full, schedule time to read through all the slips of paper. Then start over again.

Name the Furniture

Although this may seem a bit silly, it is actually an effective way to express gratitude for the people in your life. Simply walk through your house and name your furniture after people who have been important to you in some way or another. For example, name the sofa Billy, after the man who taught you to read. Or name the coffeemaker Sarah, after the woman who installed your internet service. As you sit on the sofa or use the coffeemaker, think of the person for whom it is named, and express gratitude that they have been in your life.

Three I See...

For this exercise, you will make a list of things you are grateful for, moving through your senses. Three things you can see, three things you can hear, three things you can smell, three things you can touch, and three things you can taste. You can say these things out loud, think about them, or write them down. There is no wrong way to complete this exercise. Simply take a few moments to be grateful.

Meditation

Meditation is another excellent habit to build into your daily routine. Meditation can help relieve stress, reduce anxiety, and help you be more connected to your thoughts and feelings, your surroundings, and those around you. There are several ways to practice meditation. Some methods involve religious practices, while others do not. Try the following exercises to begin meditating and discover what works best for you.

Body Scan

Begin by getting in a comfortable position. You can sit or lie down, but choose a place where you will be free and uninterrupted. The point of this exercise is to scan the different parts of your body and notice how you are feeling. You can move from head to toe or from toe to head—just move in a logical pattern and make sure you focus on all of your main body parts. Once you are settled, take a deep, intentional breath. Choose where you are going to start and focus on that body part. For example, if you are going to start with your feet, pay attention to your toes and your feet. Focus in on them and take a moment to notice how you feel. Do you have any aches or pains? Are your joints stiff at all, or do you feel anything that is uncomfortable? When you are finished focusing on your feet, take another intentional breath, and then move on to your ankles. Next, focus on your calves, and then your knees, and so on, until you reach the top of your head. When you are finished, take one more intentional breath, and then take a few final moments to express gratitude for your body and all that it can do.

Picture It

In this exercise, you will take a vacation in your mind. To begin, sit or lie down in a comfortable position. Close your eyes and take three intentional breaths. Next, picture a place that you would like to visit. It can be anywhere you choose. Perhaps you love the outdoors, and so you picture the ocean or a mountain trail. Or you may love the city, so you picture a bustling metropolis, full of lights, sounds, and excitement. There are no limits to where you can go, so choose a place that really appeals to you.

Once you have chosen where you want to go, imagine it in as great of detail as possible. What do you see? What are the details you notice? If you have chosen the beach, are there boats on the water? If so, what color are the sails? Or if you are in the city, are there billboards and advertisements around you? What do they say? What do they look like? Really spend time in this place. Notice the sounds, the smells, and everything around you.

Once you have fully explored the area, slowly come back to where you are now. Take three more intentional breaths, and then open your eyes. Take a few moments to express gratitude for your imagination.

Focus on the Details
For this activity, you will choose one object that you will closely examine. Choose whatever object you want to use, whether it is something of great significance to you, or something that is just convenient. Hold the object in your hands as you sit or lie down in a comfortable position. Close your eyes and take three intentional breaths. Open your eyes again and start to examine the object.

Notice the colors you see. Feel the different textures and pay attention to the tiny details. Notice the surface and then look closer. Can you see tiny fibers? Are there dents or scratches you never noticed before? Have you discovered colors you didn't know were there?

Once you have thoroughly examined the object, close your eyes again. Take three intentional breaths, and then picture the object. Try to picture all of the details you noticed when you were looking at it. See just how much of the object you can recall.

Take three more breaths, open your eyes, and look at the object one last time. What did you recall correctly? Was there anything you missed? Take a moment to express gratitude for whatever object you held in your hands, and the fact that this object helped you focus your attention.

Be Still

All you will do for this exercise is sit and be completely still for a few minutes. This is an excellent practice to help you begin meditating. It can help you get used to the idea of sitting and calming your mind, and it will help you start to relax.

You can choose to listen to music while you do this, or you can sit in silence if that is what you prefer. Find a place where you will be comfortable and sit in a comfortable position. Set a timer for three to five minutes or choose a song that is three to five minutes long. Once you begin, close your eyes and sit as still as you possibly can for the duration. Breathe normally but try not to move other than that. Don't focus on anything else other than sitting still.

When the time is up, take two intentional breaths and open your eyes. Take a few moments to express gratitude for having just a few minutes to sit and be completely still.

Wipe It Clean

The goal of this meditation is to help you clear your mind and try to create a blank slate. To begin, get into a comfortable position, close your eyes, and take three intentional breaths. Next, with your eyes still closed, picture a blank white space. If you spend a lot of time working on a computer, this blank space can be a blank document. If you are a teacher or prefer a classroom setting, the space can be a white board. If you are an artist, the space can be a canvas or a blank piece of paper. It doesn't matter what you choose; it just needs to be a clean, white space.

As thoughts come to your mind, imagine them appearing on this blank space. Notice them there, and then visualize erasing them. See the thoughts disappearing, and the space becoming white again. Repeat the process with the next thought that comes to mind, and continue to do so until you can have several minutes where the space stays blank.

When you are finished, take three intentional breaths. Open your eyes and take a few moments to express gratitude for your mind and your capacity to think so many thoughts, as well as your ability to dismiss them for the moment.

Focus on Others

It is important to remember that emotional intelligence involves not only thinking about yourself and how you are feeling, but also thinking about those around you and what they may be experiencing. Developing a habit of focusing on others will help you maintain a balance. The following suggestions are simple but meaningful ways to focus on others.

Say Hello

Have you noticed how easy it can be to go through your day without ever stopping to really connect with another person? Even if you work in a busy office and are surrounded by people, how much time do you spend truly trying to connect? It is most likely not very much.

A very simple way to connect with other people is to say one word: Hello. You don't need to stop and have a long conversation, and you don't even need to ask how they are doing. Simply say, "Hello." As you walk by a person in the hallway, say hello. If you pass someone in the grocery store, say hello.

Taking one second to say hello will help you acknowledge the people around you and will increase your awareness of others. It will also most likely catch them off guard, and they will have a pleasant addition to their day.

Try Something New
Another excellent way to begin focusing on others is to try something new. Consider something that you have never done before, and do it. While you are experiencing it, talk to those around you. Ask questions, or ask for advice. Spend just a small amount of time talking to those who are familiar with the activity. This will not only help you learn more about what you are doing, but will allow you to get to know people outside your normal circle. As you create a habit of stepping outside your comfort zone, your life will become richer and fuller, and you will be much more aware of all types of people.

Here are some activities to consider:
- Volunteer at a community event.
- Attend a religious service.
- Shop in a very specific store, such as sports memorabilia, craft supplies, or outdoor activities.
- Take a class.

Explore the News

It is easy to get lost in the big news stories. They dominate the television and radio programs, they cover the front pages of newspapers and magazines, and online sites offer tidbits of information to grab your attention. While it is helpful to know the major events taking place around the world, this habit is about taking a few moments every day to explore the news that is not garnering as much attention.

Seek out local news and smaller publications, and learn about what is going on in your local community. As you hear news stories, look beyond what this means for you and how this will impact your life. Stop for a moment to consider what the people are experiencing. Look at their photos and take note of their emotions.

No matter what news story you pay attention to, look beyond just the facts that are presented and focus on the people involved. Consider the victims in a crime story, appreciate the helpers during a disaster, and celebrate any good news you happen to hear.

Downtime

It is very easy to fall into the trap of being constantly on the go. There is always something to take care of and always something that needs to be done. Although this is simply the way things are in today's world, it is not good for you. It is not good for your body to be constantly on the go, it is not good for your mental health, and it is not good for your emotional intelligence. Create a habit of having some downtime every day. Although it may seem a bit contrary to schedule in downtime, the reality is that if you are not intentional about it, it most likely will not happen. The following activities will help you carve out time.

Schedule It

This first activity may seem like the simplest thing to do, but it can be the most difficult to actually accomplish. When your list of things to do gets longer and longer, oftentimes, the first thing to go is time for yourself. Make a commitment to not let that happen. Block off time in your schedule, and then treat that time the same way you would treat any other meeting or appointment.

When it is time for downtime, there is only one rule: do whatever you want to do. That's it. If you feel like taking a walk, take a walk. If you want to read, then read. There is nothing you absolutely have to do in this time, other than doing whatever you want. Do something you enjoy, and make sure it is something that will leave you feeling refreshed.

Get Away

There may be times when the only way you can actually get a break is to get away from your surroundings. This doesn't mean you have to tough it out until you can get a prolonged vacation. This means that you need to get away right now, even if it is just for a few moments. Take a quick walk outside or go for a drive. Run an errand if you need to, or perhaps just go and sit in another office or conference room for a few minutes. Simply find a way to get out of your immediate environment. Relax as much as you can, and enjoy being away.

Alone Together

A fun way to ensure that you are getting the downtime you need but still spending quality time with your loved ones is to start the practice of being alone together. All this means is finding solitary activities that you enjoy, but that can be done in the presence of another person. Perhaps it means you and your partner spend an hour reading every night. You are in the same room, and you are together, but you are both lost in your own books. Or it may mean that the entire family sits in a room together while each is doing their own thing. One may choose to color, one may wish to play games on a computer, and one may simply choose to sit and do nothing. This allows everyone to have time to themselves, yet no one is isolated.

Review

These are the top ten things to remember about forming habits.

1. It takes time to develop habits. The average time for a habit to develop is two months; however, some can take up to eight months to form.
2. The best way to form a new habit is to attach it to something you already do every day. For example, if you want to start drinking a glass of water every morning, put the water next to your toothbrush. Since you are already in the habit of brushing your teeth, it will be an easy addition to drink the water.
3. Once you have formed a habit, your brain starts to crave the reward that comes from completing the task. You no longer have to convince or remind yourself to do the activity. It just comes naturally.

4. When you have to skip doing something that has become a habit, you will feel off. You will feel as if something is missing, or incomplete.

5. When you want to develop new habits, it is best to focus on adding in one habit at a time. If you try to do more than one at a time, you may feel overwhelmed and might give up on everything. Make one small change at a time, and then gradually add in other habits once the new ones are formed.

6. In order to form a new habit, you have to be intentional about what you are doing. It will not happen by accident. Make time for it in your schedule, and make it a priority.

7. It is important to make it a habit to practice gratitude. This will help you become more aware of and grateful for the things that you do have, rather than focusing on things you don't have.

8. Making meditation a daily habit can help you clear and refocus your mind. It will increase your emotional intelligence because you will be more aware of what you are thinking and feeling. Practicing meditation will help you learn to tune out distractions and recognize your emotions, without judging them.

9. The best way to learn to focus on other people is to build a habit around doing so. It may be something you have to do intentionally at first, but over time it will become natural for you, and you will often do it without realizing it.

10. If you are not intentional about having time to sit and do nothing, you most likely will never fully relax. Creating a habit of resting will help you feel refreshed and allow you to better tend to your responsibilities.

Do

You have learned a lot about habits and what you should focus on. Now it is time to get to work. Make a list of the main habits that you want to incorporate into your life. Although there may be several things you would like to do, start by choosing the top five things. Once you have them in mind, prioritize them in the order you want to add them into your routine, and start making the first change. Figure out when you will add them into your routine, and make sure you have everything you need to be successful. For example, if want to start by getting up at the same time every morning, make sure you have a working alarm clock. If you want to start exercising every day, make sure you have proper exercise attire. If you want to eat vegetables every day, go shopping. Once you are prepared to start your new habit, get started.

As you continue to make changes, develop new habits, and grow, you will realize that you are gaining more emotional intelligence. Once the building blocks are in place, it is time to move on to really focusing on what is going on in and around you, and practicing the art of mindfulness. The next chapter will discuss the practice of mindfulness. You will learn what it really means to be mindful, as well as several specific exercises you can do to become more mindful.

Chapter 11: What Do I Do?
Mindfulness Practices

"Mindfulness is a way of being present: paying attention to and accepting what is happening in our lives. It helps us to be aware of and step away from our automatic and habitual reactions to our everyday experiences."
— *Elizabeth Thornton*

Learn

Emotional intelligence cannot be separated from the concept of mindfulness.

What Is Mindfulness?

The best way to describe mindfulness is that it is a type of alert meditation where you are keenly aware of what is happening around you. You are aware of how you are feeling, both emotionally and physically. You notice those around you, and you are completely present in the moment.

Why Is Mindfulness Important?

There are a lot of benefits to mindfulness. It can help you be less anxious, reduce stress, and manage your emotions. It allows you to stop and notice little things, and you can become much more aware of the good and enjoyable things you have in your life. It helps you focus on what is happening in the moment, and it is likely to help you worry less. You don't think about the past or future, you just relish in the present.

What Does Mindfulness Look Like?

Mindfulness involves being fully present in the moment. You focus on the little details, and you do not react or judge what you notice. You are aware of your feelings and thoughts, but you do not try and change them or dwell on them.

How Do I Get There?

One of the best things to remember as you start to work on mindfulness is to stop going through life and start experiencing it. Before we discuss specific mindfulness activities, let's look at the three main tenants of mindfulness: intention, attention, and attitude.

Intention

Although it would be highly beneficial and a wonderful way to experience life, it is not realistic to live in a state of constant mindfulness. Your daily life is likely full of responsibilities and distractions, and you rarely have time to stop and focus on the immediate moment. When you practice mindfulness, you need to be intentional about it. You intentionally focus on what is going on in and around you. It is not something that happens by accident. You make it a priority, and it has your full awareness.

Attention

Mindfulness involves paying attention to everything around you, exactly as it happens. You pay attention to noises you hear, sights you see, physical sensations, and emotions and thoughts that come to the forefront. You notice them and acknowledge them, but that is the extent of it. You do not judge them, you do not try and sort anything out, and you do not try to fix anything. You simply pay attention.

Attitude

As you practice mindfulness, keep your attitude open. Do not be judgmental, negative, or closed off. Be curious and ready to explore, and be positive that this exercise will benefit you and will bring you a better awareness of yourself and your environment. Finally, be kind to yourself. If your dear friend or a child were to come to talk with you and tell you everything that he or she was feeling, you would not reject them. You would not criticize them or try and minimize what they are saying. You would listen and be supportive and encouraging. Do this for yourself. Be kind to yourself. Do not limit or minimize what you notice, and do not try and stop the process. Let it happen and let yourself experience the entire process.

Mindfulness Exercises

Once you decide that you are going to be mindful, you can practice it anywhere, any time. You can take a minute, five minutes, or a couple hours to just be fully present and fully aware. However, there are also very specific exercises and activities you can do as you get comfortable with mindfulness. Setting aside specific time to do these things can help you focus on what you are doing and get accustomed to the thoughts and sensations you experience.

Getting Started

This is an exercise that you can do right now. Set a timer for three minutes. During those three minutes, intentionally focus on everything that is going on around you. Start by looking around the room or wherever you are sitting.

Notice everything you see. Notice colors, shapes, and textures. Notice subtle differences and big differences. Notice lines and patterns, and pay attention to small details. Next, notice the things that you hear. Notice the obvious sounds, and then pay attention to the more distant sounds. This could be a clock ticking or a dog barking far away. After that, pay attention to things that you feel. Do you feel the texture of the couch? Or can you feel jewelry against your skin? Now it is time for other sensations. Do you smell anything? Taste anything? Now think about what you are feeling. Are you tired? Are you relaxed? Do you feel anxious or worried about anything? Are there any thoughts that keep trying to push to the front of your mind? Take notice of all of these things. Once the timer stops, go on with your day.

Once you have done this exercise a few different times, it is time to move on to other more specific activities. Use the same tactics you used when getting started, but apply them to different and very specific behaviors.

Mindful Eating
Mindful eating is not only a good way to practice mindfulness to increase your emotional intelligence, it is also a good way to make healthier choices and even lose weight.

To begin with, choose a specific meal to practice mindful eating. Once your food is ready, sit down at the table and remove all distractions. Turn off music, and for best results, do not try to do this in the company of others. As you begin to eat, notice every aspect, sensation, and detail of the experience. As you pick up your utensil, pay attention to it. What does it feel like in your hand? What colors do you see? Is it cold? Is it warm? Does it feel comfortable in your hand, or are there rough edges?

Before you begin eating, observe the food for a moment. What colors and shapes do you see? Is there steam coming off of it? Are there different colors? What can you smell? Can you pick out the specific aromas, or does it all combine into one smell? Pay attention to these details, noticing them before you eat.

Once you take your first bite, close your eyes. Notice the flavors and textures as you chew. Are there subtle flavors, or is it just one bold taste? Can you pick out different spices? Do you notice the different flavors of vegetables and fruits? Pay attention with every bite.

As you continue to eat, pay attention to how your body feels. Are you still hungry, or are you satiated? Is the food sitting well, or are you starting to feel bloated or uncomfortable?

Finally, examine the thoughts and feelings that come to mind as you eat. Are you happy with your choice, or do you wish something were different? Are you satisfied, or is there something missing? Does this meal bring back any memories, whether they are pleasant or not? Are there any thoughts or concerns that are distracting you? Remember, do not pass judgment on any of this, simply notice and recognize it.

Try this activity with different meals and in different settings. You can even do this with something as simple as a cup of coffee or tea. It doesn't matter what you are eating. The purpose of the exercise is to be mindful during the entire experience.

Mindful Cooking

If you have a busy schedule and are trying to figure out ways to carve out time for mindfulness, mindful cooking is a good way to go. You have to make the meal anyway, so use it as a time to be mindful. Although you can be mindful no matter what you are cooking, it can be even more enjoyable if you are cooking something that involves several steps and several different ingredients.

Before you start, take a few moments to clear off your work area. This will allow you to completely focus on mindful cooking without getting distracted by other chores that need to be done. Once your area is clear, set out all of the ingredients you will use. As you do this, begin paying attention to specific details of the ingredients. Notice the colors and textures of the vegetables, take a moment to smell the different spices, and pay attention to the temperature of the meat or protein.

Once you start preparing the meal, be aware of what you are doing. As you chop vegetables, listen for the sound of the knife. Make note of the difference between the sound of the knife slicing through the vegetables, and the sound of the knife hitting the cutting board. Watch the way the vegetables move and fall. Are there specific aromas that arise as you cut the vegetables? If you are cutting onions, acknowledge the sensation of the tears as they fill your eyes or fall down your face.

As you continue to cook the food, notice the aromas change as new ingredients are added, or as the food heats up. Watch the colors change and notice the sensation in your hand as you move your spoon or spatula across the pan.

While you put the finishing touches on the meal, what thoughts or feelings do you have? Are you proud of what you have accomplished? Do you have a greater appreciation for the food that is in front of you or for the skill that you have? Does this make you want to learn to cook even more elaborate meals, or do you not enjoy the process?

Acknowledge everything you have experienced, but do not assign any judgment to it.

Mindful Cleaning

Another way to incorporate mindfulness into your regular routine is to practice mindful cleaning. This is an excellent way to make a mundane task more meaningful and can help you improve your emotional intelligence while maintaining your living space.

As with the other mindfulness exercises, mindful cleaning involves being aware of every detail and sensation as you clean. As you are getting started, choose one task to focus on. However, as you get more comfortable with the process and experience, you may want to expand it to every time you clean and even while cleaning the entire house. The benefit of this is that when you are finished, not only will your home be clean, but you will feel more relaxed and at peace.

Focus on the following questions as you clean:

- What do you see? Pay attention to the colors and textures around you. Are you using a cleaning product? What color is it? Does it make a specific pattern as you spray it on the surface? What color rag are you using? Is it smooth, or are there ridges? Do you see the dirt that you are going to be cleaning, or is this just a general clean to keep things fresh? Focus on everything you see, no matter how big or little it may be.

- What do you hear? Can you hear the sound of scrubbing or water running? Are there background sounds as you work? Can you hear yourself breathing?

- What do you smell? If you are using a cleaning solution, what does it smell like? Is it strong, or is it something you have grown accustomed to? Can you smell the water? Are things getting fresher?

- What do you feel? Are you wearing gloves? What do they feel like on your skin? Can you feel the temperature of the water through the gloves or the texture of the surface that you are cleaning? If you are not wearing gloves, what does it feel like on your hands? Is it rough or smooth? Is the water hot or cold? How does your body feel while you are cleaning? Do your legs hurt from standing, or does your back hurt? Is the room cool, or are you breaking a sweat? Notice all of the different sensations.

- What are you thinking? What comes to mind as you clean? Are you thankful that you have a home? Are you angry that you have to clean? Do you have any specific memories in this particular room?

When you have finished cleaning, take a moment to congratulate yourself for not only spending time being mindful but also for completing a chore.

Mindful Playing

Lest you think that mindfulness always has to be a solemn or serious experience, try your hand at mindful playing. To do this, choose an activity that you really enjoy doing. This can be playing with your kids, swimming, playing with a pet, or playing a sport. No matter what you choose to do, be mindful about it. Pay attention to what you are seeing, hearing, feeling, smelling, and thinking. Focus on the way you feel while you are doing the activity. Are you laughing more? If you choose to do this activity with someone else, do you feel more connected to the person? What is it that you enjoy so much about this activity? Why is it fun for you? Does it bring back positive memories?

Taking time to be mindful and fully in the moment will bring you an even greater enjoyment of something you already love to do. You will find new things to appreciate, and you will notice that you feel more relaxed and fulfilled than you normally do.

Mindful Strolling

If you want to get some exercise and fresh air while practicing mindfulness, consider mindful strolling. Choose a place where you can walk as slowly as you would like without having to worry about traffic. Make sure that you feel safe and secure, so that you can truly focus on what is happening.

As you begin to walk, start by focusing on the feeling of your feet as they hit the ground. Is the surface stable and smooth, or is it a rocky terrain? Listen to the sounds you hear as you step down. Are there leaves crunching, or do you shuffle your feet a bit? Next, notice the feeling in your legs. Notice the way your muscles move and pay attention to the way all of your joints move. Continue to move up your body, paying close attention to the physical sensations as you walk. Do you swing your arms, or are they still? Do you feel the blood rushing to your fingers, or do your hands brush the sides of your legs? Are your shoulders hunched forward, or do you hold them back and stand tall? Take deep breaths, paying attention as the air fills your lungs.

Once you have spent time focusing on the physical sensation of walking, notice your surroundings. Make note of all of the different colors that you see, and the way that one tree can have a wide range of shades and colors. Listen for the sounds around you, whether it is birds in the distance, leaves rustling in the wind, or an insect buzzing around.

Finally, zero in on what emotions you are experiencing while you walk and what you are thinking. Are you tired? Do you feel lonely? Have you enjoyed having the time to yourself? Has this walk brought up any memories for you? What are you aware of or experiencing during this time?

Remember not to judge the things you notice. Just be aware of them and acknowledge them.

Review

These are the top ten things to remember about mindfulness.

1. Mindfulness is a vital tool when you are trying to build your emotional intelligence.
2. Mindfulness helps keep you in the present, where you can focus on what is happing at this very moment, rather than dwelling on the past or worrying about the future.
3. Mindfulness has been shown to help reduce stress and anxiety. It helps you get a clear perspective on what is happening in your life and can help you make better decisions.
4. As you practice mindfulness, it is important that you do not assign judgment to what you are thinking or feeling. Acknowledge your thoughts and recognize your emotions, but do not judge them.
5. In order to practice mindfulness, you have to be intentional. Mindfulness does not happen on accident. Your tendency is most likely to go about your day, taking care of all of your responsibilities, without stopping to really focus on what you are doing. You have to be intentional about stopping and being mindful.
6. Mindfulness takes your attention. The practice involves paying attention to everything around you, even down to the smallest details.
7. As you practice mindfulness, make sure that you keep an open and positive attitude, and that you are kind to yourself. Mindfulness should be an enjoyable experience, and one that you look forward to.

8. Mindfulness can take as long as you want it to. Whether you choose to spend one minute, ten minutes, or two hours, you will experience the benefits and clarity that comes with being mindful.

9. You can incorporate mindfulness into your everyday chores. Being mindful while you cook or clean can help you better enjoy the task and can give you a new appreciation for what is around you.

10. It is important to take time to be mindful while you play or have fun. Intentionally focusing on being present and in the moment while you are doing something enjoyable will only enhance the experience.

Do

As you have learned in this chapter, you have to be intentional about being mindful. Right now, decide what activity you are going to do. Choose the time and place, and stick to that commitment. Once you do it the first time, you will see how beneficial and enjoyable it is, which will make it easier to do it the next time.

As you continue to grow and improve yourself, you will undoubtedly notice that more often than not, you are your own worst enemy. You will criticize yourself, doubt yourself, and become a stumbling block to your own growth. The next chapter will focus on the way to combat this issue, and the final aspect of strong emotional intelligence: positive self-talk.

Chapter 12: What Do I Do? Positive Self-Talk Practices

"Positive thinking will let you do everything better than negative thinking will."
— Zig Ziglar

Learn

Although you may not be aware of it, you talk to yourself all throughout the day. Sometimes it may be very intentional and you say specific things. Other times it may be a thought running through your mind, although you are not conscious of it. Regardless, it happens, and it has a profound influence on you. If your self-talk is negative, your outlook will be negative, and you will be limited in what you can do and achieve. If your self-talk is positive, your outlook will be positive, and you will be more successful. It is essential to develop positive self-talk practices.

What Is Positive Self-Talk?

In the very simplest terms, positive self-talk is telling yourself positive, encouraging, and uplifting things. Rather than focusing on mistakes you have made, you focus on the things that you have done right. When you do mess up, you don't chastise yourself but instead look for ways that you can learn and grow. You do not limit yourself, but you tell yourself that you can achieve your goals.

Why Does Positive Self-Talk Matter?

Studies have shown that self-talk has a profound impact on your emotional health and can even make a difference in your physical health. When you engage in negative self-talk, you will suffer. You will increase your stress and anxiety levels, and you will limit yourself. Some examples of negative self-talk include the following statements:

- "I can't do this." If you tell yourself you can't do something, you have already given up. Rather than pushing forward and trying to find solutions to the problem, you have decided that you are unable to do the task at hand. You have no reason to try, and you believe that it is something you can never master.
- "I keep messing up." Everyone makes mistakes. It is part of life, and it is how we learn and grow. However, if you tell yourself this every time you make a mistake, you are actually giving yourself permission to continue making the same mistakes. It is as if you are accepting them as the norm rather than focusing your attention on how you are going to do better in the future.
- "I am a failure." If you tell yourself you are a failure, you are condemning yourself to never being able to achieve your goals. Rather than viewing your mistakes or failures as separate incidences, you have assigned them as part of your identity. Once this happens, you stop trying.
- "No one will find me attractive." If you tell yourself that no one will ever be attracted to you, you will stop trying to make yourself look good. Although there is much more to life than appearance, the truth is that it

does matter. Appearance plays a role in almost all of your interactions. If you start to believe that you will never be considered attractive, what is the point of trying to become more attractive? Why should you make an effort if you believe it is futile? By telling yourself this, you actually limit yourself.

- "I can't lose weight." Telling yourself this is a sure sign that you have given up. Rather than focusing on the specific barriers you may be facing and trying to find ways to overcome those barriers, you have determined that it is never going to happen.

Learning to practice positive self-talk will make an impact in every area of your life. You will make better and healthier choices, have less stress and anxiety, and find that you are reaching your goals. It will improve your relationships with people, as you will have more self-confidence and self-worth. It is an indicator of strong emotional intelligence and will dramatically improve your life.

What Does Positive Self-Talk Look Like?

Positive self-talk involves saying things that build yourself up, encourage you, and inspire you. Following are some examples of positive self-talk:

- "I am working on improving myself. This is not easy, and I am proud of myself for putting in all of the hard work." This statement allows you to realize that you are not perfect and that there is always room to learn and grow; but rather than focusing on your shortcomings, you are focusing on the fact that you are moving forward. You should be proud of yourself because what you are doing is not easy, but you are doing it still.

- "I continue trying to master this task. It takes courage to keep trying, and I am learning something every step of the way." It can be frustrating when you make mistakes. That is normal, and you don't have to pretend that everything is going well if it isn't. But how you frame and handle those disappointments makes all the difference in the world. Recognizing that your repeated attempts take courage will inspire you to keep trying. Knowing that you are learning something along the way will give you a reason to keep learning. You won't give up because you recognize the value in the process.

- "I am free to make my own choices." Knowing that you are free and that you have control over the choices you make will keep you from feeling like you are trapped or are a victim. You will know that only you decide what you do and don't do, and that you are responsible for what comes your way.

- "I am significant." There may be people or experiences in your life that have left you feeling as if you are not significant. You need to know that this is not true, and you need to remind yourself of this frequently. You are significant. Knowing this will make a difference in the way you approach your life, and the way you interact with other people in your life. You will keep moving forward and keep making strides to become the best version of yourself, because you know that you can and will make an impact.

- "I am highly capable. If there is a skill that I don't have, I have the ability to learn something new." Approaching things with this mindset will give you the freedom to really try anything. You know what you can do, but you also know that even if you lack certain knowledge or skills, you are capable of learning. You won't approach any situation feeling intimidated or unable to handle what comes your way. You will have an open mind, give it your best effort, and will most likely find much more success and happiness along the way.

- "I am enough." Once you come to accept the truth that you are enough, you will stop trying to prove yourself or earn the praise and acceptance of other people. Rather than improving yourself to make people like you, you will make changes because you know that it is the best for you. You will feel strong and competent, and this will have a positive impact not only on your life, but also on the lives of those around you.

- "I am worth it." You have undoubtedly learned that increasing your emotional intelligence and working on yourself is not easy. It can be uncomfortable and force you to examine your thoughts and emotions. However, if you realize that you are worth it, you will keep moving forward. You will put in the hard work of exercise or make healthy decisions about food. You will set aside time for yourself and really make it a priority because you will realize that you are truly worth it.

- "I cannot control other people. I can control myself, and I will control myself and put the best version of myself out there." There are always going to be people in your life who are trying to take you down. It's not a pleasant thought, but it is the truth. There are people who are going to insult you and put you down, and you may even encounter people who hurt and abuse you. If you come to accept the truth that you cannot control other people, and that you can only control yourself, you will find more freedom in even the worst of circumstances. You will not blame yourself for the mistreatment you receive because you realize that you are not responsible for their behavior. You will not try to change anyone, because you know that the only one you can control is yourself. This gives you freedom and permission to worry about yourself and your behavior without getting caught up in other people's thoughts, perceptions, attitudes, or actions.

How Do I Get There?

To begin developing positive self-talk, you need to be intentional about it, and you need to recognize negative self-talk when it happens. Be aware of what you are saying to yourself and look for ways that you can turn the negatives into positives.

Positive Self-Talk Practices

Try the following practices to increase your positive self-talk. Although it may seem awkward and uncomfortable at first, it is worth the effort, as it will have a profound impact on your life.

Let Your Mirror Talk

Your mirror is something that you look at every day, and in this exercise you take full advantage of that fact. All you need to do is get a dry-erase marker. Now, write positive messages to yourself on the mirror. Write down your goals, along with encouraging notes of how you will achieve those goals. Remind yourself that you are worth all of the hard work, and that you are fully capable of handling whatever comes your way.

Whenever a negative thought comes into your head, counter that thought with something positive, and then write the positive talk on your mirror. Take time to read the messages on the mirror every day, at least twice a day. When you are getting ready in the morning and when you are getting ready for bed at night, read what you have written there. Let those words sink into your mind.

Listen to Yourself

For this exercise, you will make an audio recording of the positive messages that you want to focus on. This can be things that you want to tell yourself or encouraging quotes that you hear or read. Compile a list of the things that you want to hear every day. Once you have all of the messages, use the voice memo setting on your phone and record yourself reading these things. Then, listen to the recording every day, preferably a few times throughout the day. You can do it while you are exercising, before bed, or when you are driving in your car. It does not matter when or where you do it—the point is to hear yourself saying kind and positive things to yourself. It will help you in the moment, and it will also make it easier to have positive self-talk throughout the day because you will grow accustomed to hearing positive statements from yourself.

Take Five

For this exercise, you will only focus on five things at a time. At the beginning of the week, make a list of five things that you like or appreciate about yourself. There are no parameters to this. You can list physical attributes, things you have accomplished, or personality traits. Whatever you choose, write them down. You can write them down on a piece of paper, type them into your phone, or combine this with an earlier exercise and write them down on your mirror. After you write them down, read them aloud. This is important because not only are you reading the positive things about yourself, but also you are speaking them aloud. Your brain is hearing you say it, and the more you hear it, the more it will become engrained in your consciousness. Read this list aloud every morning and every night, and make a new list at the beginning of each week.

Review

Here are the top ten things to remember about positive self-talk.

1. Self-talk has an impact on every aspect of your life, including your mental and emotional health. You engage in it all day, every day, whether you are aware of it or not.
2. Negative self-talk can increase your levels of stress and anxiety. You do not have a hopeful outlook, and you can begin to feel trapped and in a rut. The more you tell yourself negative things, the more you will start to believe them, and the cycle will continue.

3. If you continually tell yourself negative things, you will stop trying to achieve your goals. You give up, limit yourself, and believe all of the bad things you say about yourself.

4. Positive self-talk not only impacts your life, but also has an impact on your relationships and the lives of those around you. You will feel better and more confident which will be evident to everyone who interacts with you.

5. If you start labeling yourself in negative terms, you will accept that as part of your identity and will stop trying to make positive changes. You will accept that you are a failure or that you just can't do something, and then there will be no reason to keep trying.

6. Having positive self-talk does not mean ignoring anything negative. It means accepting that things are going to go wrong, but also accepting those things as challenges and realizing that you are capable of handling whatever comes your way.

7. You need to be intentional about incorporating positive self-talk into your life. As you start to pay attention to the things you say to yourself, you will very likely realize that you regularly say things that limit you or make it more difficult for you to keep trying.

8. It is important to also hear yourself saying positive things as well as just thinking about them. The more you hear it, the more you will start to accept it as truth. You have most likely spent the majority of your life speaking to yourself in a negative manner, so you will have to undo that habit and create a new way of thinking.

9. One of the most important things that you can tell yourself is that you are worth all of the hard work that it takes to make lasting, positive changes in your life. There are going to be times when you want to give up and wonder if it is worth it. If you have been telling yourself that *you* are worth it, you will start to believe it, and you will keep moving forward.

10. Another very important concept for you to accept is that you cannot control other people. You cannot control what they say or what they do. You are not responsible for their actions, and you cannot cause them to do anything or not do anything. All you are responsible for is what you do. You control how you respond or if you choose not to respond. You don't need to worry about what others think of you, and you do not need to try and earn their approval. Simply keep moving forward, focus on what you need to do, and let others do whatever they are going to do.

Do

It is time to get started on the positive self-talk. To begin, choose one thing that you like about yourself right now. It does not have to be elaborate—just choose something positive that you can focus on. Say it out loud and repeat it throughout the day. Set an alarm on your phone for every ninety minutes. When the alarm goes off, repeat the positive aspect out loud and then go on with your day. This is a very simple and easy thing to do, but it will have an impact.

Once you have focused in on the one attribute, choose which of the other activities you are going to focus on and get started. The activities are simple and do not take much time, so if you wanted to, you could do all of them now. Whatever you choose to do though, get started.

Finally, as you go through your day and negative thoughts come to mind, recognize them. Stop yourself from going down that road, and replace the negative statements with positive ones.

Now that you have learned what you can do to increase your emotional intelligence and are actively making strides to do so, let's take just a few more moments to consider how all of this can apply to children. You are undoubtedly aware that children struggle with a lot of the same issues that adults struggle with, including self-doubt and negative thoughts. Children can learn how to increase their emotional intelligence, so let's see what will work for them.

Chapter 13: Does It Work for Children?

"You have to write the book that wants to be written. And if the book will be too difficult for grown-ups, then you write it for children."
— Madeleine L'Engle

Learn

Children need to learn how to identify, understand, and manage their emotions. This will not only help them better control their behavior now, it will also help them as they grow into adulthood. Studies have shown that children who have developed a high level of emotional intelligence also tend to have higher than average overall intelligence and often perform better on standardized tests. They tend to have stronger relationships and are better equipped to handle the changes that often come as they get older.

How Children Develop

Before taking a look specifically at how children develop emotionally, it is important to have a general understanding of how children develop. Although there are several different theories of development, two of the most common are the theory of psychosocial development that Erikson developed and the theory of cognitive development that Piaget developed.

Erikson's Theory of Psychosocial Development

Erik Erikson identified eight different stages to describe the way a person grows and develops through life, focusing specifically on conflicts that a person will encounter, as well as different types of social interaction. Erickson's stages include:

- Stage 1 – Trust versus Mistrust. This stage occurs during infancy. It is during this time that children learn whether or not they can trust the people around them. They are entirely dependent on someone else to meet their needs, and it is during this stage that they begin to realize who will help them, and who will not.

- Stage 2 – Autonomy versus Shame and Doubt. This stage occurs during early childhood, usually between the ages of eighteen months and three years. It is during this stage that a child begins to learn what things he or she can do for themselves. They begin to be less dependent on their parents, and want to try to do everything. This includes activities such as getting dressed, choosing what they want to eat, and learning to use the toilet. If a child has a difficult time learning how to be independent or is not given the opportunity to learn how to be independent, he or she will likely struggle with feelings of self-doubt and may feel inadequate.

- Stage 3 – Initiative versus Guilt. This stage occurs between the ages of three and five. During these years, children begin to learn that they can take control of situations, and at times can direct other people. This is often seen in the form of children taking responsibility for directing games and activities. Children often use their imaginations to take even more control, creating characters, scenes, and scenarios that must be followed. If children are not allowed to direct and have influence over others during this time, they can begin to feel guilty and incapable, and will very likely become highly dependent on other people.

- Stage 4 – Industry versus Inferiority. This stage typically take place when a child is between the ages of six and eleven years old. During this time of their lives, children are becoming more and more aware of their friends and other people who are around them. They also become more aware of their own accomplishments, and begin to take pride in the things they can do. As they interact more with their peers, children at this stage often begin to compare themselves to those around them. If they feel others are more capable, they may start to feel insecure. If they feel they are stronger than others, they may have a boost of self-confidence.

- Stage 5 – Identity versus Role Confusion. This stage occurs when children are between the ages of twelve and eighteen. It is during this stage that children develop their sense of who they are, how they fit into society, and start to recognize their purpose. It is during this time that children will experiment with different attitudes and identities, trying to figure out who they really are. They may move around between different groups of friends and try out various activities, all in an attempt to find out what works for them. If children are not allowed to do this, they may never really know who they are. They will not know what makes them unique, and they will often struggle with self-confidence and self-esteem, as they will be confused as to who they really are. Children who are not allowed to experience and master this stage will very likely have troubles with commitment as they get older. They never learned to commit to an identity, belief system, or group of friends, and they will tend to struggle with commitment throughout the entirety of their lives.

- Stage 6 – Intimacy versus Isolation. This stage occurs when a person in the early stages of adulthood, and continues until around age 40. It is during this stage that a person looks to find a stable, lasting, intimate relationship. This does not only mean romantic relationships, but also applies to friendships and familial relationships. For those who are unable to form intimate relationships, they will find themselves isolated. They will be unable to truly connect with other people, and will often struggle with intense feelings of loneliness.

- Stage 7 – Generativity versus Stagnation. This stage occurs between the ages of 40 and 65. This is the time of life when people are trying to create things that will have a lasting impact and are looking for a way to leave a legacy. If someone is unable to find a way to do this, he or she will usually find that they are stuck. They will be very self-centered and will find that they do not have deep or meaningful relationships, as they are unable to think outside themselves.

- Stage 8 – Integrity versus Despair. This stage begins at about the age of 65 and continues until a person dies. During this stage, people look back on their lives and wonder if they have made a difference or lasting impact. For those who are able to look back on their lives and feel as if they have made a lasting impact, they often feel a profound sense of peace and contentment. They feel as if they have been successful, and also feel that they have attained wisdom, which they can pass on to younger generations and make even more of an impact. For those who do not feel as if they have made a difference, they will fight feelings of bitterness and regret, and they will battle depression and the idea that they wasted their lives.

Although each stage that Erikson identified contains very specific goals, each one also involves a wide range of emotions. Children who can develop a healthy amount of emotional intelligence will be better equipped to navigate through all of the stages of development.

Piaget's Theory of Cognitive Development

Jean Piaget formed the theory that children's intelligence will change as they grow, and that they go through four different stages of development.

- Sensorimotor Stage – A child is in this stage from the time they are born until they are between eighteen months and two years old. During this stage, a child's mind is growing rapidly, and their cognitive abilities are dramatically increasing. The child begins to understand the world around them, and is able to make connections between their senses and actions. For example, they learn that if they bring their hand to their mouth, they can get food, or they can suck their thumb. This stage is broken down into six separate stages:

147

- o Reflex Acts – During this stage, which occurs from birth to about four weeks, everything the child does is a reflex. For example, if you put something in their mouth, they will suck.
- o Primary Circular Reactions – This stage occurs from one month to four months of age. During this time, a baby will do things simply because it brings them pleasure. For example, they will suck on their fingers because they like the way it feels, or they will wiggle their hands because they like the sensation.
- o Secondary Circular Reactions – This stage is from the age of four months to eight months. During this stage, a baby will repeat actions with different objects, just because it brings them pleasure. For example, a baby will rub a soft blanket because they like the way it feels, or they will shake a rattle because they like the sound.
- o Coordinating Secondary Schemes – In this stage, from ages eight months to twelve months, babies learn how to use the things that they have learned in order to reach a goal. For example, if a baby wants to reach a toy that is behind another object, the baby will reach out and move the object in order to get to the toy.
- o Tertiary Circular Reactions – This stage is typically between the ages of twelve and eighteen months, and it involves voluntary actions by a baby in order to learn or explore.

For example, a baby in this age will take a toy apart, and then try to put it back together.

- ○ Symbolic Thought – This final stage of the sensorimotor stage occurs between the ages of 18 and 24 months. This is when children begin to be able to visualize things, even when the things are not in front of them. This includes the idea of object permanence, when a child knows that an object is still there even if they cannot see it. For example, before a child recognizes the concept of object permanence, if a toy is placed under a blanket, the child will think the toy has disappeared and will not look for it. However, when a child does recognize the idea of object permanence, if a toy is put under a blanket, the child will move the blanket in order to keep looking for the toy.

- Pre-Operational Stage – This stage occurs between the ages of two and seven years. During this time, children are able to think symbolically, but they are not yet able to think operationally. This means that they do not use logic to help separate or combine ideas. Children in this stage tend to have a difficult time focusing on more than part of a situation at a time, or more than one part of a social setting at a time. Children have also not yet developed the ability to think beyond themselves. They view every situation as to how it will affect them, and they believe that everyone thinks and feels the exact same way they do.

- Concrete Operational Stage – This stage occurs when children are between the ages of seven and eleven. It is during this time that children begin to have more rational thoughts and develop logic. They have not yet learned to fully think abstractly or hypothetically. Children learn how to classify objects, and learn about the concept of conservation, realizing that when liquid is poured from one container to another, the amount of liquid stays the same, even though the size and shape of the container may be different.
- Formal Operational Stage – This stage occurs from the ages of twelve and up. During this stage children learn to think abstractly. They develop the ability to solve math problems in their head and to consider hypothetical situations.

As children grow and learn, they also begin to process emotions.

How Children Process Emotions

Children are born with the capacity to experience emotional reactions. They cry, feel hungry, get frustrated, and feel pain. As they get older, they learn more about their emotions and are able to assign words to the things they are feeling.

Although some emotions develop over time and in different cultural environments, researchers believe that there are eight emotions that everyone is born with. These emotions are:

- Anger
- Fear

- Sadness
- Joy
- Surprise
- Interest
- Disgust
- Shame

Children understand and experience these emotions in different ways, depending how old they are.

Infants

Infants do not have the capacity to make rational decisions about their emotions, and instead are acting and reacting to stimuli. For example, if they feel hungry, they cry. If they are pleased by something, they laugh. If there is something they don't like, they will pull away or try to avoid it. On the other hand, if there is something they do like they will lean toward it and try and engage. Infants are also capable of soothing themselves.

One way to help infants is to play music for them. Studies have shown that music can help reduce stress for infants. Upbeat and repetitive music is actually more soothing than lullabies. Classical music can also soothe an infant while stimulating their brain.

Toddlers

As infants grow, they learn to understand more about their emotions and feelings. Children as young as one can be taught simple sign language, which allows them to communicate ideas they cannot express verbally. This helps reduce tantrums and meltdowns, and allows children to identify their needs.

Parents can help their children develop emotional intelligence by discussing different emotions and helping them name and identify different feelings. For example, if a character in a television show is angry, parents can say, "That person seems upset and is acting like they are angry. Why do you think he is so angry? What do you think he can do about being angry?" Although the toddler will not give a long and complex answer, it helps them learn to recognize emotions in others, as well as in themselves.

Elementary School
By the time children are in elementary school, they have learned to identify all of their primary emotions, and are beginning to experience and understand secondary emotions. They are often learning to process complex ideas such as:
- Regret
- Guilt
- Satisfaction
- Resentment
- Jealousy
- Hope

Children in elementary school can engage in different activities to help them regulate their emotions. They can identify what they are feeling, draw pictures to help express themselves, and can even practice simple mediation and mindfulness exercises.

Parents can help their elementary school-aged children by not only having them identify their emotions, but also by having them identify what triggers the different emotions. For example, if they are sad, don't just have them say how they are feeling, but ask them why they are sad. Try to get to the bottom of why they are experiencing the emotion.

Middle School

Middle school is a time of profound change for children. These changes occur physically, mentally, and emotionally. With the onset of puberty, hormones surge, and everything in their life is in flux. Also, during this time, children began to make more and more of their own choices. They tend to pull away from their parents a bit and ask for more privacy than they did when they were younger.

Because of all of the changes they are enduring, children in middle school tend to start viewing themselves differently. They may start to wonder where they fit in and who they are. As they consider their emotions, they begin to contemplate what their different feelings say about them as a person, and they wonder if they are the only ones to feel such emotions.

High School

It is during the high school years that children really start to discover who they are. They want to be able to establish themselves apart from their parents. They examine what they believe and who they really want to be. During this time, they can be heavily influenced by their peers, as they are trying to discover exactly where they fit in.

Emotionally, children are learning to identify and validate their feelings. The inconsistency and intensity of emotions that were common during puberty have started to level off, and children begin to address the "why" behind what they are feeling. They start to put their feelings into context and can really start to understand the methods of controlling their emotions.

High school is also the time when children are able to start understanding the feelings of those around them. Once they have established who they are and have more security in their own identity, they are able to look beyond themselves and to other people. They begin do develop more empathy.

Habits for Children

No matter the age of the child, there are habits they can develop that will help them increase their emotional intelligence. If they start developing these habits at a young age, as they grow and mature, they can go deeper with their thoughts and exploration of their emotions.

Put a Label on It

An effective way for children to develop their emotional intelligence is to learn to recognize emotions in other people. This can begin at a very young age. Have a child look at a picture book and ask them to identify what they think the different characters are feeling. Ask them questions such as, "Do you think this person is sad, or happy?" or "How do you think this person feels?"

You can also do this by having them watch a movie or television show with the sound off. Frequently press pause and ask the child what they think the character on the screen is feeling.

Once they are able to label the feelings, ask them why they think the character feels that way. You can then have them consider how they would feel if they were in a similar situation.

For older children, direct their attention to background characters in movies. Point out someone who is observing the action and ask what they think that character may be feeling and why. This will help the older child begin to consider the emotions of those who may not be the center of attention. They will begin to consider everyone around them, not just those who are the most obvious.

Express It

Another activity to help improve emotional intelligence in children is to have them simply express what they are feeling. Do this at a variety of times, not just when the child seems upset about something. The conversations do not need to be long or drawn out—simply ask the child to give one sentence, or even one word, to describe how they are feeling.

For younger children, expect simple emotions such as, "I feel happy," or "I feel sad." As the children get older, their emotions will grow more complex.

This exercise will help children begin to learn that it is okay to talk about their emotions. It will help them get more comfortable with whatever they may be feeling, and can also help them learn that emotions are nothing to be ashamed of.

Draw It

Give a child a blank piece of paper and ask them to draw a specific emotion. Do not give them any other directions, just allow them to be creative and decide how they wish to express the emotion. Some may choose to draw a person expressing that emotion, while others may choose to draw scenarios that make them feel that way. Still others may choose colors and strokes that seem to evoke that feeling.

This activity helps children grow more comfortable thinking about different emotions and exploring how the emotions can be expressed. It gives them a safe way to consider the different aspects of emotions, and can help them better identify these feelings in themselves and others.

Identify the Good

It is important for children to learn how to have positive self-talk. If they can develop this habit when they are young, it will be much easier for them to carry it on into adulthood. Have a child write down five things that they like about themselves. If they are not yet able to write, have them tell you the things and write it down for them. Have them read the statements aloud every day for a week. At the end of the week, have them choose five other positive statements for the next week. Continue this practice throughout the year.

Habits for Parents and Caregivers

While it is helpful for children to learn to implement daily habits in order to build their emotional intelligence, there are also habits that parents and other caregivers can adopt in order to help children learn.

Model It

Children look up to you and are going to learn by watching the things that you do. Make sure that you are making your own emotional health and intelligence a priority. Model positive self-talk, speak freely and openly about emotions, and do not pass judgment on your own feelings.

Identify It

When you see a child exhibiting a particular emotion, help them identify the emotion. For example, if a child is throwing a tantrum, rather than just getting frustrated with the child, help put a label on what they are feeling. You can say, "It seems as if you are angry," or "Right now you are acting as if you are frustrated." You can also ask a child what they are feeling, in a very specific manner. Rather than saying, "How do you feel?" you can ask, "Are you feeling sad?" or "Are you excited?" Children will hear the names of the emotions and associate them with what they are feeling.

Empathize

Although it can be frustrating when a child is throwing a temper tantrum, it is important to find a way to validate what they are feeling and show empathy. Rather than simply correcting the behavior, take a few moments to acknowledge what they are feeling. You could say something such as, "I know it is frustrating when you don't get to have what you want," or "I know you are sad that you have to go to bed." This helps the child realize that what they are feeling is valid, and they will not feel that they are wrong for expressing their emotions, nor will they feel ignored or dismissed. You still may need to correct behavior, but try to do so in a way that addresses the behavior while still validating the emotions. For example, "I know you are sad and don't want to leave the park, but running away from me is not safe. What is another way you can tell me you are sad?"

Make Talking Normal

If you want to be able to have in-depth and emotional conversations with your child, especially as he or she becomes a teenager, you need to make talking normal from a very young age. Set aside time to talk every day. Talk about the little things which will make it easier to talk about the big things when you need to. It doesn't need to be a long and drawn-out conversation, especially if that is not typical for your family. That may make your child feel awkward and unwilling to open up. Find a time when everyone is together, such as after a meal or just relaxing in the evening, and instigate small conversations. You may want to try some of the following ideas to get started:

One Word

Ask everyone in the family to choose one word to describe their day. Although at first it may seem as if this will limit the conversation to one-word answers, you will most likely be surprised at how much this gets your child talking. You can ask why they chose that one word, or they may have a difficult time choosing just one word, leading to more conversation about what they experienced during the day. You can set the example of giving your one word, and then explaining why you chose that word.

High and Low

Have everyone share the high point of their day, and the low point of their day. As you begin this exercise, you can expect that the answers will not be very deep, and that is okay. Let the child go as deep as they wish. As the child gets more and more comfortable sharing, you will likely see that there will be times when their answers are very deep and will reveal what they are truly thinking or feeling.

If I Could Design It

For this activity, tell everyone in the family that they are given the power to design exactly what their life looks like. Where they live, what they do, what they look like, etc. Then have them tell you what life would look like. This is not only a fun way to get everyone talking, but can give you valuable insight into what your child values and enjoys.

If I Were A...

Choose a category and have everyone complete the sentence of what they would be in that category. For example, "If I were a vegetable, I would be..." Once they choose what they would be, ask them why they made that choice.

As you have these conversations with children, remind them that there are no wrong answers, and that they never have to apologize for what they are thinking or feeling. Do not push them to go deeper, just listen and enjoy the talking. Let the conversation go where it goes.

Review

Here are the top ten things to remember about how you can help children begin to build their emotional intelligence.

1. Recognize that children learn different concepts at different stages. Understand where children are at in their development, and help them regulate their emotions according to their abilities.
2. There are eight basic emotions everyone is born with: anger, fear, sadness, joy, surprise, interest, disgust, and shame.
3. As children grow older, they begin to develop more complex emotions such as regret, resentment, and hope.
4. Music has been shown to help soothe an infant.
5. Toddlers experience deep and strong emotions but do not have the vocabulary to express what they are feeling, and this often leads to tantrums. Teaching a child basic sign language can help the toddler communicate better and feel less frustrated.
6. When children are in elementary school, they can begin to identify what triggers some of the different and more complex emotions they are experiencing.
7. The middle school years are very tumultuous for children, as everything in them is changing, and their friends are changing, too. During these years, children need to be reassured that what they are feeling is normal and what they are going through is normal.
8. High school is the time when children not only begin to better understand and regulate their own emotions,

but they are also more aware of the emotions of those around them and begin to develop empathy.

9. Helping children learn to improve their emotional intelligence will help them throughout their entire life. It can improve their performance in school, their social relationships, and even their athletic ability.

10. Parents and caregivers can play a vital role in helping children develop their emotional intelligence. This is done not only by helping children learn to talk about their own emotions, but by adults modeling healthy emotional intelligence in their own lives.

Do

Again, the most important thing you can do to help a child understand their feelings is to model emotional intelligence in your own life. Talk openly about emotions and help them see that feelings are nothing to be ashamed or afraid of.

Make a regular habit of checking in with children and seeing how they are doing emotionally. Reassure them that they can talk openly and honestly, and give them plenty of affirmation for being truthful about how they are feeling.

Now that you have finished learning all of the material, it is time to review what you have learned and begin to take your next step.

Conclusion

"In literature and in life we ultimately pursue, not conclusions, but beginnings."
— *Sam Tanenhaus*

Final Thoughts

Although it is a relatively new field of study, you have undoubtedly learned that emotional intelligence has a profound impact on your life. As it involves your self-awareness, self-management, social awareness, and social skills, it will play a role in every area of your life. Once you learn to accept your emotions without judgment and to see and accept the emotions of those around you, you will notice a profound difference in your life.

Appreciate the way that your brain operates, and recognize that the ability to experience a wide range of emotions is a gift. It can improve your creativity, your relationships, and the way you experience life.

Perfection Is Not the Goal

As you begin to try the different activities in this guide, remember that the goal is not perfection. Not only is it impossible to be perfect, the point is not to change your actions, but to develop a greater understanding of your emotions and the emotions of others. If you simply focus on changing your behavior without learning to connect more with your emotions, you will find that, although you are going through the right motions, you are no more connected with your emotions than when you started.

Do What Works for You

Finally, make sure that you are doing what works best for you. You have been given several ideas to get you started. Try them out and see what helps you. If there is something that doesn't work or doesn't fit in with your lifestyle or personality, do not feel as if you need to force it. Simply move on to another activity.

Realize that what you are doing is valuable and difficult. It is worth all of the hard work that you will put into it.

www.ingramcontent.com/pod-product-compliance
Lightning Source LLC
Chambersburg PA
CBHW060232030426
42335CB00014B/1425